# EASY, EASIER, EASIEST

# TAILORING

## by

## pati palmer & susan pletsch

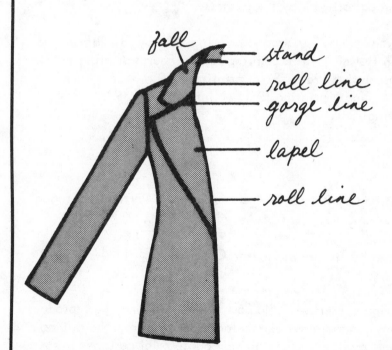

fall
stand
roll line
gorge line
lapel
roll line

*cover & illustrations by Priscilla F. Lee*

Whenever brand names are mentioned, it is only to indicate to the consumer products we have personally tested and with which we have been pleased. We are not subsidized by anyone. There may very well be other products that are comparable or even better to aid you in your sewing or that may be developed after the printing of this book.

A special thank you to our innovative friend, Marta Alto, and to our families who have been supportive fans.

Technical artwork by the authors.

Copyright© 1977. Second printing 1978 by Pati Palmer and Susan Pletsch. Third printing 1979. Fourth printing 1979. Fifth printing 1980. Sixth printing 1980. Seventh printing 1980. Eighth printing 1981. Ninth printing 1981. Tenth printing 1981.

Published by Palmer/Pletsch Associates, Portland, Oregon U.S.A.

Printed by The Irwin-Hodson Company, Portland, Oregon U.S.A.

Book inquiries may be sent to Palmer/Pletsch Associates, P.O. Box 8422, Portland, Oregon 97207.

ISBN 0-935278-03-6

About the authors . . . . . .

Pati Palmer and Susan Pletsch, two talented home economists,
have developed careers promoting a favorite hobby, home
sewing. They have co-authored four sewing books, have es-
tablished their own publishing company, and now travel across
the U.S. teaching seminars based on the Palmer/Pletsch books.
They also consult with the fabric and notions companies. Their
most recent accomplishments include designing patterns for
Vogue and McCall's and creating and
starring in an educational film based
on a Palmer/Pletsch book.

Pati Palmer

Pati and Susan met as educational
representatives for Armo Co., a
shaping manufacturer. Pati has
also been Corporate Home Economist for an Oregon department
store, as well as buyer of sewing
notions. Pati graduated from Ore.
State University with a B.S. in
Home Economics. She is active in
the American Home Economics Association, Home Economists in Business, and Fashion Group.

Susan Pletsch

Susan has been a home economist
with Talon Consumer Education,
where she traveled extensively
giving workshops. She was also
a free-lance home economist
with many sewing related firms.
Susan graduated from Arizona State University in home economics and taught home economics to special education students.
She is active in the American Home Economics Association
and Home Economists in Business.

Pati and Susan are individually recognized for their sewing
skills and teaching and lecturing abilities. Together they
produce an unbeatable combination of knowledge, personality
and talent.

# Table Of Contents

# Tailoring is <u>EASY</u>!

Can you believe it? We have the nerve to call tailoring EASY! And we mean it. We began as you did, "Me tailor? Heavens no - that's too hard for me!" But tailoring can be as easy as <u>you</u> want it to be. That's what this book is all about.

We've written a book full of choices. You must evaluate your time, talent, patience, budget, and wardrobe plans and then choose tailoring methods to meet your needs. So you can be a snob and "custom" tailor if that is your choice. But you will also find some sneaky, speedy ways to have a great look-ing blazer in 1/4 the time with 1/4 the hassle. Using the "Easiest" methods, we can crank one out in 8 hours - and YOU can too!

Read the entire book first! Then...<u>think</u> positively, your new blazer is going to make Calvin Klein think he needs sewing lessons! <u>Decide</u> which methods meet your talents and needs. <u>Plan</u> your work so that it will progress smoothly and rapidly. Then <u>smile</u> and pat yourself on the back. Isn't tailoring easy!

# What Makes it "Tailored"?

   "Tailoring" is a method of sewing that makes a garment more durable than traditional dressmaking. It generally applies to coats, jackets, and blazers - those garments that cost more to buy or sew - those garments we must wear for several seasons. "Tailored" can also refer to a "man-tailored" fashion look (crisp details, masculine fabrics, man's suit styling) which can be found on anything from skirts to dresses to pants.

   A blazer, which we define as a type of jacket that always has a lapel, a rolled collar, and a straight, uncuffed sleeve, contains virtually all of the traditional techniques that set tailoring apart from dressmaking. You may find one or more of the following tailoring techniques in a tailored jacket or coat, but if you want to learn all about tailoring, make a blazer - it has them all!

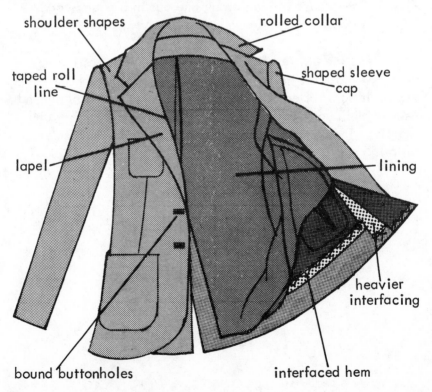

shoulder shapes

rolled collar

taped roll line

shaped sleeve cap

lapel

lining

heavier interfacing

bound buttonholes

interfaced hem

# Why Learn Tailoring Techniques?

1. If you learn to tailor, all of your sewing will improve because you will have tried and succeeded with the psychologically most difficult sewing project. It's much like the novice skier who dares to tackle the advanced slope and succeeds – she must put forth maximum effort and use every bit of previous training and knowledge. From that point on, skiing is a breeze!

2. You can make your sewing time as profitable as possible by making only those things you can't afford to buy. Susan says she can afford $8.00 T-shirts but refuses to spend $200.00 for the quality blazer she loves. She multiplies the cost of the blazer ingredients by 7 to come up with the approximate cost of a comparable ready-to-wear garment. With $40.00 worth of ingredients you can produce a $280.00 blazer – a savings of $240.00! Tailoring can save tons of money!

3. Special tailoring techniques can be used for super effects in sewing many other garments. For example, the taping technique taught on page 55 can be used to prevent "gaposis" on the V-neck of a daring evening dress. See the "Tailoring Techniques ... Other Uses" section for more specifics.

# Let's Define: Easy, Easier, Easiest

CUSTOM - Included in this book to compare "slow torture" hand methods with contemporary techniques. In traditional custom tailoring:
- an underlining is optional
- interfacing is hand tailor basted or pad stitched to the garment.
- the best quality fabrics are suggested since this will be a much prayed-over garment

Advantages: Subtle, durable, shape with all fabrics.
Disadvantage: Very slow but can be worth every painful stitch.

EASY - Easy tailoring is one step faster than custom--machine stitches replace most of those done by hand.
- uses an underlining
- the interfacing is machine stitched to the underlining
- lapels are hand padded

Advantages: Faster than custom, durable--great for children's coats; can use a budget hair canvas such as P-26 or Hymo; can use a quality hair canvas for superior shaping without the stiffness of a fusible.
Disadvantages: Underlining plus interfacing may be too bulky or firm for some fabrics.

EASIER - Aaah! Fusing replaces stitches!
- uses an underlining
- no hand pad stitching
- interfacings fused to underlining

Advantages: Speedy, yet gives extra body, a way to use fusibles on any fabric without creating ridges on outside or altering the fabric surface--a way to use fusibles with seersucker!
Disadvantages: Underlining plus interfacing may be too bulky or firm for some fabrics.

EASIEST - The fastest method possible!
- no underlining
- no machine or hand pad stitching
- interfacing fused directly to fashion fabric

Advantages: SPEED!
Disadvantages: May make fabric too firm, leave a ridge on outside where interfacing ends, or interfacing may separate or bubble if NOT fused properly.

10

# How to Make a Blazer in 8 Hours!

Pati is a super speedy seamstress who can make a blazer in 8 hours - but Susan (who usually sews at a snails pace) can now make that 8 hour blazer too. Here are some secrets:

1.  Select a basic pattern and plan to make it several times in different fabrics - each time you repeat a pattern it goes together faster and more easily.
2.  Look for these pattern features that are fast:
    - patch pockets instead of welt
    - no back or sleeve vent  (or stitch existing ones closed)
    - lining (faster than finishing seams in an unlined garment)
    - pattern must include a lining pattern
    - jiffy patterns can be deceptive. They claim to be easy because there are fewer pattern pieces which means fewer seams, but...more darts. We feel that sewing and pressing darts is not necessarily faster AND if you have fitting problems, the more seams you have to work with the easier to fit.
3.  Use no-fail, easy-to-tailor fabrics (see page 17 for details). Look for these in order of speed:
    - polyester double knit (fastest)
    - wool or polyester/wool double knit
    - wool tweed
    - linen-like fabrics
    - linen

    Be sure to avoid (for an 8-hour blazer only!):
    - lightweight wool flannel (shows wear quickly)
    - velvets (harder to sew and take forever to press)
    - tightly woven permanent press fabrics (tend to pucker and are hard to ease)
    - plaids of any type (look great but take longer to cut and match)
4.  Fastest methods:
    - fusible interfacing fused directly to fabric
    - machine buttonholes
    - fused hems

# Think Coordinates - Sew an OUTFIT

Spend more time but get better value from your time spent – don't just make a jacket or coat – make an outfit!

## Save Time

1.  Make a two-piece outfit – That is, make a grey blazer and grey skirt or a camel coat and pants. There is super classic fashion in a monochromatic ensemble and definitely extra wardrobe mileage.
2.  Go one step further – make a blazer, vest, skirt and pants out of the same fabric. This four part wardrobe can yield a minimum of six combinations.
3.  Go even further – make two four-piece outfits out of a year-round fabric like a stretch woven polyester in two compatible colors (such as camel and navy), and you can interchange all the parts. The two outfits then yield over 25 combinations. Pati always has these two colors in her wardrobe and builds all other garments around them.

NOTE: When you make a two, three or four-piece outfit, make the "other pieces" (vest or skirt or pants) first to become familiar with the fashion fabric -- how it presses, how it sews.

## Save Money

1.  On fabric – by buying enough fabric for a 3-piece outfit, you can often make the fourth piece for free because of improved cutting advantages.
2.  On other clothes – fewer blouses, shirts and sweaters will compliment more outfits.
3.  On accessories – when you have all those compatible pieces you can wear the same shoes, handbag, scarves and jewelry. (This also means you save time in shopping for your accessories).

NOTE: Carry color swatches with you! Buy one of those plastic accordian-fold wallet photo holders for swatches and favorite pattern yardage requirements. Look at it every time you make a fabric or accessory purchase and slap your hands if it doesn't fit into the "grand scheme of things". See illustration on previous page.

# Pattern Selection

1. Select a pattern with good lines for you. Some hints:

| To make you look shorter and wider | To make you look taller and more slender |
|---|---|
|  |  |
| double breasted, wide lapels, straight bottom | single breasted, narrow lapels, rounded bottom and deep "V" lapel (one or two button jacket) |
|  |  |
| short, boxy style (a la Chanel!) | long jacket with princess seaming |

Remember, almost any style will add height and be slenderizing if the jacket and pants (or skirt) are in the same color and fabric.

NOTE: ALWAYS look at the line drawings on the pattern or in the pattern book as they will give you the true shape of the fashion. We love Vogue Pattern Magazine for all the line drawings in the last five or ten pages. It's a nice home catalogue.

14

2. Two "easy lines."

| Easier to fit | Easier to sew |
|---|---|
| 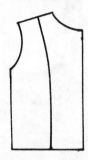 |  |
| This style is easy to fit in shoulder and bust areas. Simply adjust seams until it fits. | A one piece pattern is psychologically easier for some people. |

3. Buy the right pattern size (see fitting section).

4. Before you buy the pattern--check the guide sheet. If the pattern does not have a lining pattern included, don't buy it. It is harder to finish off all those seams so that they look pretty than to line a jacket, and cutting your own lining is a hassle. (If the back of the pattern envelope gives a yardage requirement for lining, a lining pattern is included.)

5. After you buy the pattern--pin the tissue pattern together and try it on - an easy way to see if the style is good for you (see page 43). If it is not, we feel it is better to waste the $5 pattern than to waste all your fabric and time on something that won't be flattering.

6. If a roll line is not marked on the pattern, it will be more difficult to tailor properly. You may buy a new pattern (we would - ugh!), or pin collar to pattern and try it on. When gorge line lies flat and smooth - crease, and that becomes the roll line. Fortunately, most patterns have a roll line marking.

# Choose a No - Fail Fabric

If it's worth doing, it's worth doing right! So invest in this tailoring project. Spend as much for fabric as you can possibly afford. You will be repaid immediately with easier cutting and sewing, and super looking, long wearing fashion.

The No-Fail Fabric Chart was designed to show sewability at a glance. If you want a hassle-free fabric choose one from the "Easiest" column. These will sew and press quickly with professional results. Those in the "Easy" and "Easier" columns require a bit more skill but can still be painless.

Since your fabric choice will help determine the sewing methods you will use, Easy, Easier and Easiest also relate to shaping techniques described on page 33. So the fabrics in the "Easiest" column are the easiest to handle but also the easiest to tailor because they may be used with the fusible interfacing to fabric method. But as always--FUSE A TEST SAMPLE FIRST! Easy and Easier tailoring methods may be used with either Easy or Easier fabric columns because both use interfacings applied to an underlining.

We believe in mentioning brand names wherever possible to help speed up your shopping. Your favorite store should have the same or a comparable fabric. We have personally tested these and know they perform well.

## NO-FAIL FABRIC CHART

| Easy | Easier | Easiest |
|------|--------|---------|
| wool gabardine | wool flannel | wool flannel (heavy) |
| suit weight silk | stretch-woven | wool tweed |
| corduroy | polyester | linen |
| velveteen | short staple stretch- | synthetic linen |
| washable velvet | woven polyester | polyester or |
| seersucker | linen-like fabrics | wool double knit |
| cotton chintz | heavy cottons | Ultrasuede |
| heavy coatings | | denim |

# WOVEN FABRICS

WOOL GABARDINE (by Anglo and Stevens) - If you're looking for a medium weight solid color wool, choose gabardine over flannel - gab resists wrinkles and wears much better. Gabardine is a lovely hard-surfaced fabric made from long wool fibers, but it is not "Easiest" because of that hard finish. It shows press marks easily so requires very careful pressing and sewing to avoid an overworked appearance.

WOOL FLANNEL (by Anglo and Pendleton) - if you decide to use a flannel, use a good one. Anglo makes a heavier weight gorgeous flannel called Aristoc (used by Anne Klein in ready-to-wear).

WOOL TWEED (Pendleton and Hamilton Adams' Booth Bay woolens) - This is one of the best "first project" fabrics - tweed hides sewing and pressing goofs.

HEAVY WOOL COATINGS (Mazerak by Anglo is lovely!) - Custom methods are best, plus follow all suggestions for eliminating bulk. Hold your shears at an angle to bevel all cut edges。

SEERSUCKER - Remember to fuse to an underlining - fusing directly to seersucker flattens the puckers you just paid for!

COTTON CHINTZ - Use prints only, solid colors show every little pucker and press mark.

HEAVY COTTONS - Choose a print to help hide sewing and pressing inaccuracies in heavy cottons or cotton blends.

DENIM - Look for a soft denim. Stiff ones are hard to tailor because the crispness and the tight weave resists easing.

SUIT WEIGHT SILK - Be sure to underline for strength and body.

LINEN & SYNTHETIC LINEN - Linen pants or skirts should be underlined to minimize wrinkling, but learn to think of them as posh status wrinkles - you're wearing the real thing. Moygashel linen is popular. Moygashel also makes a beautiful Fibro rayon called Moymacrae that is close in weight to linen. It is Pati's favorite Spring/Summer fabric and is also used extensively by designers like Anne Klein.

18

**LINEN-LIKE FABRICS** (Pontoon, Icebound) - Because these are lighter weight and more loosely woven than the other linens mentioned, they should be underlined or have interfacing fused to an entire piece from edge to edge.

**STRETCH-WOVEN POLYESTERS** - Best investment for year-round dressing and always looks crisp and fresh.

**SHORT STAPLE STRETCH-WOVEN POLYESTER** (Steeplechase by Burlington/Klopman) Short fibers produce a wool-like hand in this innovative fabric.

## NAPPED FABRICS

**CORDUROY** - Buy the best quality possible to make the garment worth the time invested.

**VELVETEEN** (by Crompton) - The key is to choose a quality one for best wear and wrinkle resistance. Susan has a print velveteen blazer by a designer underlined with a hair canvas for wrinkle resistance and loves it!

**WASHABLE VELVET** (Matinee' by Martin) - We would normally not recommend you tailor on velvet, but the new ones - a blend of cotton and rayon - are unbelieveably easy to sew and press. Technically they are a velvet but look and handle like a very rich velveteen.

**ULTRASUEDE**® (by Skinner) - Tailors amazingly easily but requires special sewing techniques. See Sewing Skinner® Ultrasuede® Fabric by Pati Palmer and Susan Pletsch.

## KNIT FABRICS

**POLYESTER DOUBLE KNIT** (Ponte Plus by Milliken) - Visa finish makes this fabric cooler and more resistant to stubborn stains. Polyester knits tend to resist pressing but their stability and durability make them popular.

**WOOL DOUBLE KNIT** (18 oz. by Anglo or Pendleton is super!) The heavier weight 18 oz. is really a best buy - this fabric is easier to sew and shape.

# Sometimes a Great Notion

Have these sewing aids on hand at all times--especially for tailoring! See referenced pages for more about "how to use".

| GADGET | USE | PAGE |
|---|---|---|
| **Cutting and Marking Aids** | | |
| 1. Pins (long glass head) | Pins thick fabrics easily | 53 |
| 2. Sewing gauge (6" ruler) | Marks hems & button-holes | |
| 3. Sharp shears (long, bent handle) | Smooth, even cutting | |
| 4. Pinking shears | For seam finishing | 72 |
| 5. Embroidery scissors | Ripping/clipping/snipping | |
| 6. Tracing wheel (smooth-edged) Tracing paper (washable) | Speedy marking | 53 |
| 7. Tailors chalk (with holder) | Easily removed marking | |
| **Sewing Aids** | | |
| 1. Talon Basting Tape | Double-faced sewing tape, stick-bastes | 122 |
| 2. Belding Lily Tape-Stitch | Premarked sewing tape for accurate top-stitching | 123 |
| 3. Sobo Glue | Liquid glue for glue-basting underlining and interfacing | 30 |
| 4. Baste & Sew Glue Stik™ | Glue stick for glue-basting | 68 |
| 5. Singer "Yellow Band" sewing machine needle | Prevents skipped stitches | 123 |
| 6. Pointer/Creaser | Turns corners right side out | |

## NOW ORGANIZE THESE GADGETS:

1. Hang a mug rack on the wall - the handiest way we have found to store all "grab-for" items. Tie a pretty ribbon loop on items that don't want to hang.

2. Find a small chest of drawers to put next to the machine for storing small supplies and pressing equipment.

3. Keep an organizer tray on your machine for small items that won't hang on the mug rack.

4. Hang a bulletin board above the machine to hold pattern pieces, guide sheets, hand needles.

5. Pin a paper lunch bag on the ironing board and tape one to the machine for scraps and threads - we hate to pick up threads!

NOTE: A FREE organizer -- if you sew next to a window with a curtain, pin your pattern directions to the curtain so they are easy to find and follow.

# Learn to Press

## PRESSING EQUIPMENT

Don't even consider making a tailored garment unless you have (or are willing to purchase) some basic pressing equipment. The absolute essentials are:

1. Seam roll - a sausage-shaped gadget used to press open flat seams and cylinders like sleeves and pant legs. The seam allowances fall over the edge of the roll and allow your iron to touch only the stitching line itself.

2. Pressing ham (tailor's ham) - a ham-shaped surface ideal for pressing curved and shaped areas, helps give "people shape" to flat fabric.

3. Point presser/clapper - a wooden combination tool used to press open seams and points, and to flatten a seam by holding steam in a fabric. Often used with a seam roll or ham.

4. Steam iron - look for one with lots of holes. We like the "shot-of-steam" types with an extra button to push for a jet of steam that will press even the most stubborn fabric.

There are some fantastic pressing aids that we love for tailoring and hope you will try. But these are <u>optional</u>.

1. <u>June Tailor's Tailor Board</u> - the most versatile pressing tool. This marvelous thing has several "can't live without" surfaces. The long curved edge is perfect for pressing open a curved collar seam, or blazer front. Small curve just fits rounded collars or cuffs, and the point presser end is the best way to press into collar points.

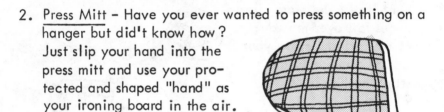

2. <u>Press Mitt</u> - Have you ever wanted to press something on a hanger but did't know how? Just slip your hand into the press mitt and use your protected and shaped "hand" as your ironing board in the air.

3. <u>See-Through Press Cloths</u> - a sheer press cloth that allows you to see what you're pressing and still protect the fabric.

4. <u>June Tailor Velvaboard</u> - a super new item! It holds steam in a unique bristled pad, then reflects it back into napped fabrics to steam press without flattening the nap.

NOTE: Fingers are a FREE pressing tool! You can slightly finger press a seam or dart in the right direction BEFORE permanently pressing with the iron or pounding block. Great for top pressing.

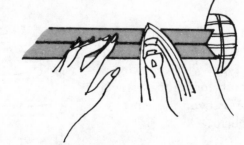

## PRESS AS YOU SEW

"Press as you sew" has been preached for years, but no where is it quite as important as in tailoring. Please don't think you can ignore pressing and pay your cleaners to press after you've finished. Cleaners can often do a nice final press - but how can they possibly get inside your jacket after it's completed? So move the ironing board next to your sewing machine, adjust the board to machine table height, and then sew, swivel, press, sew, swivel, press.

1. Press with an "up and down" motion of the iron whenever possible, otherwise slide iron along seam in ONE direction in order to make a smooth seam.
2. Use lots of steam.
3. Press on the wrong side. Use a press cloth if fabric is heat-sensitive.

## HOW TO PRESS: A Seam

1. Press seam as it was stitched to remove any puckers, and to blend stitches.

2. Place seam over seam roll. Saturate with steam by holding iron 1/8" above fabric surface.

3. Place point presser/clapper on top of seam and apply light pressure. The clapper used to be called a pounding block because fabrics were actually pounded into shape, but today's fabrics just need gentle pressure, not a beating!

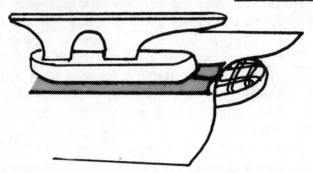

4. Top-pressing in our book is fine. Most pressing should be done from the inside to prevent possible shine, but do top-press when construction pressing hasn't quite done the trick. Saturate with steam, then fingerpress.

NOTE: Pressing takes PATIENCE!! Too-speedy pressing can create an overpressed, shiny, "I'm old and worn" look in a new garment. Synthetic fabrics will overpress more quickly than natural fabrics because the fibers are more heat-sensitive, so use a very light touch with these.

HOW TO PRESS: A Finished Edge with Enclosed Seams

This applies to seams in collars, faced fronts, lapels, and curved necklines. Trim and clip where necessary. Press seam as it was stitched. Carefully press seam open over seam roll, ham, top of point presser, or tailor board, (whichever is the best fit). Then press to one side and understitch if necessary. Fold to finished position and final press.

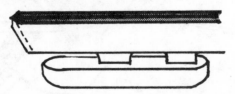

## HOW TO PRESS: A Dart

Press dart as it was stitched to flatten fold line and to blend stitches together. Place the dart over the appropriate curve of the ham and tuck paper under fold to prevent an indentation from showing on the right side. Steam. Flatten with point presser/clapper.

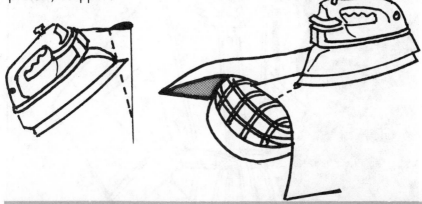

NOTE: The ham has many curves on it - one for every part of your body. Bust darts go over the very round curve at edge of hams skirt darts over a flatter curve on top surface of ham.

Hints for Darts:

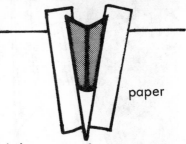

1. If dart is bulky, clip open and put strips of paper under edges to prevent press marks on right side. Press.

paper

2. Vertical darts are pressed toward the center for consistency.

3. Horizontal darts are pressed up. We're not just trying to be different, we think this gives a smoother, higher-busted younger look.

NOTE: Press lightly - If it isn't flat enough at first then lightly press again. And again. And again. Much better than too much the first time for a shiny, old look.

27

# The Critical Issue - Shaping Fabrics

Tailoring is the last holdout in the "let's eliminate all that inside stuff" movement - and for good reason. The shape in a tailored garment is really "the thing". We use much more subtle shaping and use easier methods than in years past, but the need for support and strength for that fashion fabric hasn't changed.

Here are the layers as they relate to tailoring in order of application:

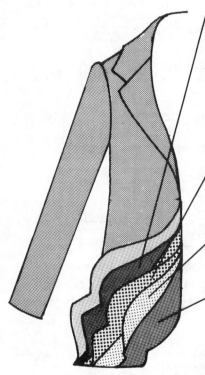

Underlining - Provides shape, body and support to large areas of a garment; for example, the body of a coat would be underlined, the collar interfaced. An underlining can also be a "cheat layer" to hold markings, make hems invisible, a place to tack interfacings and facings.

Interfacing - A generally firm fabric that is used to provide shape, body and support in small areas (edges and details) in a garment.

Interlining - A lofty layer of fabric stitched inside a garment to provide added warmth.

Lining - Fabric cut from separate pattern pieces that is assembled and then stitched inside the garment to cover the inside construction and to allow the garment to slide on and off easily.

## UNDERLINING

Choose underlining fabric by the amount of body needed to create the look you want from your fashion fabric. As fashion changes from shaped to softer silhouettes you may still want to use an underlining - it will make light colored fabrics opaque, and will allow you to use speed techniques (like fusing) on fabrics that otherwise would not accept them.

How to Underline :

Basting an underlining in place is tedious and not always accurate. There is too much chance for the underlining to slip while sewing. What is the answer? SOBO GLUE! Sobo is a liquid fabric glue that dries fairly clear and soft. It can be found in most sewing and notion departments.

Underlining and interfacing is simple -- if you glue with Sobo!

1. Place your fabric on a flat padded pressing surface. Steam press all the wrinkles out.

2. Place your underlining on top and press the two together. This removes wrinkles and any possible shrinkage. Lift underlining and dot Sobo glue on fashion fabric close to the edge in seam allowances. Pat the two layers together. Allow 5 minutes to dry.

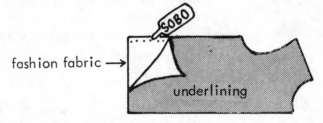

fashion fabric →

underlining

3. For more underlining information, including the "Glue and Fold" technique, see Mother Pletsch's Painless Sewing, by Pati Palmer and Susan Pletsch.

## HOW TO CHOOSE AN INTERFACING:

Place your fashion fabric on top of your interfacing and feel the two together:
1. The interfacing should compliment the fashion fabric, not overpower it.
2. The two fabrics should be care-compatible.
3. Try draping the two to a shape that resembles the place where they will be used together. For example, fold them around your wrist to resemble a cuff.

Remember that tailoring is different:
1. Tailored garments receive greater strain due to more frequent wear. We would interface the hem of a coat, but not necessarily the hem of a dress.
2. When in doubt – interface. Your clothing will look better and wear longer. No matter what interfacing you choose, the garment will look better than if you used nothing.

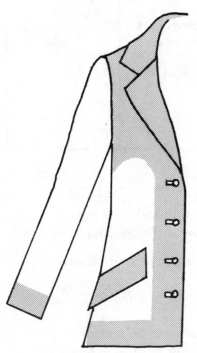

### WHERE TO INTERFACE :

Edges – (armhole, neck, front, hem) because edges are subject to excessive wear and interfacings provide strength, body, and stretch-prevention in these areas.

Details – (collar, cuff, pocket, band) because the fashion details of a garment should be a positive fashion statement – a firmly shaped collar, a crisply tailored belt, and pockets that won't droop.

| INTERFACING/UNDERLINING WEIGHT CHART | | | |
|---|---|---|---|
| | Stitchable Interfacing | Fusible Interfacing | Underlining |
| Light-weight (LW) | Armo-Press<br><br>Veriform Durable Press | Fusible Feather-weight Pellon<br>Lightweight Easy Shaper<br>Sof-Shape fusible Pellon | Poly-SiBonne Plus (Stitchable)<br><br>Poly-cotton batiste |
| Medium-weight (MW) | Acro (only light-colored hair canvas)<br><br>Bravo | Midweight Fusible Pellon<br><br>Suitweight Easy Shaper<br><br>Suit Shape<br><br>Armo-Weft<br><br>Mediumweight Pel-Aire | Veriform Durable Press (Stitchable)<br>Fuseaknit (Fusible)<br><br>Easy-knit (Fusible) |
| Heavy-weight (HW) | Armo P-1 (Fino II)<br>Armo P-26<br><br>Hymo | Fusible Acro<br><br>Heavyweight Pel-Aire | --- |

Now use the Fashion Fabric/Shaping Fabric Chart to put the right interfacing and underlining with your fashion fabric. Find your fabric on the chart, select your tailoring method (see reminder listing below), and then simply use the shaping fabrics as listed.

Custom - Hand stitch interfacing to an underlining or directly to fashion fabric.
Easy - Machine stitch hair canvas to an underlining - hand pad stitch lapels.
Easier - Fuse a fusible interfacing to an underlining
Easiest - Fuse interfacing directly to fashion fabric.

## FASHION FABRIC/SHAPING FABRIC CHART

| Fabric | Method | Interfacing | Underlining |
|---|---|---|---|
| 1. Wool gabardine/ Light flannel | Easy | HW Stitchable | LW Stitchable |
| | Easier | HW Fusible | LW Stitchable |
| 2. Suitweight silk/ chintz/ seersucker | Easier | MW Fusible or HW Fusible | LW Stitchable |
| 3. Corduroy/ velveteen/ washable velvet | Easy | HW Stitchable | LW Stitchable |
| | Easier | MW Fusible or HW Fusible | LW Stitchable |
| 4. Heavy coatings | Custom* | HW Stitchable | --- |
| 5. Wool tweed/ heavy flannel | Easy | HW Stitchable | LW Stitchable |
| | Easier | HW Fusible | LW Stitchable |
| | Easiest | MW Fusible | --- |
| 6. Regular or short staple stretch-woven polyester | Easy | MW Stitchable | LW Stitchable |
| | Easier | MW Fusible | LW Stitchable |
| | | HW Fusible | LW Stitchable |
| 7. Linen-like fabrics | Easy | MW Stitchable | MW Stitchable |
| | Easier | HW Fusible | LW Stitchable |
| 8. Heavy cottons/ denim Linen/synthetic linen | Easy | MW Stitchable | LW Stitchable |
| | Easier | HW Fusible | LW Stitchable |
| | Easiest | MW Fusible | --- |
| 9. Polyester double knit/wool double knit | Easier | MW Fusible | LW Stitchable |
| | Easiest | MW Fusible | MW Fusible |
| 10. Ultrasuede® | Easiest | MW Fusible | --- |
| | | HW Fusible | --- |

*Custom Method is suitable for any fabric listed, but essential with heavy coatings that would be too bulky with an underlining or a fusible interfacing.

33

## STITCHABLES VS. FUSIBLES

| STITCHABLES | FUSIBLES |
|---|---|
| Even though we highly recommend fusible interfacings, there is still a place in fine tailoring for stitchables. Because a fusible becomes somewhat firmer after application, a stitchable may give you a softer more subtle shape and can be used with all fabics. | We suggest fusible interfacings wherever possible. They give the best look in the least time and least amount of hassle, even for the inexperienced. They are especially nice with knit fabrics and they are an outstanding help in any area you plan to topstitch. They firm up the area so your topstitching is smooth. Fusibles get firmer after fusing. For example, the filler is left out of Fusible Acro, so it is soft when purchased, but will get firmer after fusing. |
| From now on think of the stitchables as the GLUEABLES. You can glue them in place instead of basting. | |
| Stitchables get softer after use, especially washing. See page 62 for stitchable interfacing applications. | Our Easier and Easiest methods use fusibles exclusively. |
| Custom and Easy methods rely on stitchables for a subtle look. | |

## GENERAL FUSING INSTRUCTIONS

Read and follow the manufacturer's instructions first. If unavailable, then:

1. Preheat iron, set on "WOOL" setting.
2. Fuse for 10-15 seconds per section without sliding iron.
3. Use firm, two-handed pressure.
4. Use a press cloth. (Damp-if your steam iron doesn't steam like crazy!)

NOTE: Use a minimum of 10 seconds to fuse any fabric. The heavier the fabric, the more seconds you should use. Susan uses the MISSISSIPPI trick. Count one Mississippi, two Mississippi, etc. You will then be sure to count 10 full seconds.

# HOW TO CUT AN INTERFACING WITHOUT A PATTERN

## Interfacing a one piece Front or Back

If your pattern does not include an "all-in-one" interfacing piece, you may use your front and back pattern pieces to cut your own interfacing. Draw interfacing cutting line on pattern with a Flair-type pen.

FRONT: Interfacing should extend 2 1/2" below armhole, 4" across front, and include 1" of bust dart.

NOTE: Front interfacing may be cut above the bustline (without a dart) as in other garments, but you get a better shape in the bust area when cut as illustrated. Besides...it keeps the boobies warm!

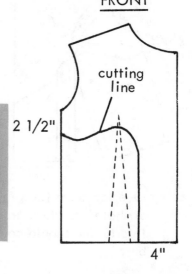

FRONT

cutting line

2 1/2"

4"

BACK: Interfacing should be cut 2 1/2" below armhole, 6-8" below neck and should be cut on fold.

NOTE: An easy way to cut an interfacing...cut outside edges first. Take a sharp pencil and poke through your pattern on interfacing cutting line every 1" or 2". Remove pattern from fabric and cut following pencil dots.

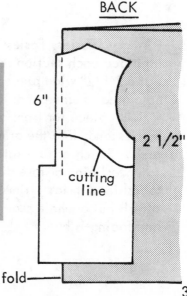

BACK

6"

2 1/2"

cutting line

fold—

1.  For Custom method, use an "all-in-one" interfacing for superior shaping.

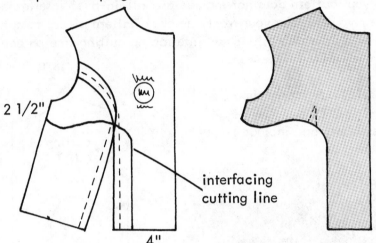

2 1/2"

interfacing cutting line

4"

Overlap seam lines in armhole and chest area. Interfacing should cover bust.

Mark dart on interfacing where seamline spreads apart.

2.  For Easy, Easier, Easiest methods interface each section separately. Cut a 2 1/2" wide piece for armhole area of side panel and a 4" wide piece for front panel that extends into the armhole area. Stitch or fuse interfacing to underlining or fuse directly to fashion fabric. Trim 5/8" off all but armhole seam if interfacing is bulky.

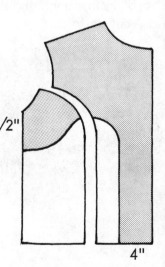

2 1/2"

4"

## INTERLINING

An interlining is the layer that adds extra warmth to a coat or jacket. These fabrics should add warmth but not weight, so look for a lightweight but lofty fabric. Some suggestions:
1. Armo Wool - a loosely woven wool - dry clean only
2. Pellon Polyester Fleece - a washable non-woven fleece
3. Outing flannel - a washable cotton or cotton/polyester flannel (be sure to preshrink!)
4. Ti-Rite (Armo) or Tri-Shape (Stacy) - lofty woven washable polyester/rayon lambs wool

Some lining fabrics are interlinings also:
1. Pre-quilted fabrics
2. Millium - an insulated lining
3. Fleece-backed lining

The easiest way to interline is to stitch the interlining to the lining - in other words, to underline the lining! Since the interlining occupies some of the inside ease, it is usually placed in the body of the garment but not the sleeves.

To interline:
1. Cut interlining from lining pattern pieces, omitting back pleat and hem.
2. Baste center back pleat in lining closed. Pin corresponding lining/interlining pieces together and machine baste all edges 1/2" from edge.
3. Assemble lining as pattern suggests.
4. Trim bulky interlining close to stitching line.
5. Stitch lining into garment as directed on page 99.

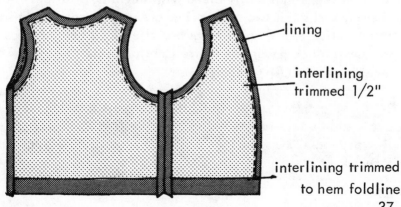

lining

interlining trimmed 1/2"

interlining trimmed to hem foldline

37

# LINING

The finishing touch – the lining layer – can be as gorgeous or as functional as you want it to be. A lining should cover the inside construction, so an opaque fabric is important; a slick fabric makes putting on and taking off the garment easier; a lining fabric should be as long-wearing as the fashion fabric (relining a jacket or coat is NOT FUN!) See page 99 for lining methods.

For functional purposes, we really like polyester linings – they wear forever, are easy to handle, and maintain their shape well. Some suggestions:
1. Ciao – polyester crepeon by Armo
2. AlaCreme – lightweight polyester satin by Skinner
3. Coupe de Ville – lightweight polyester woven fabric from Burlington/Klopman
4. Lutesong – medium weight woven polyester satin by Skinner
5. Crepe Radiance – a medium weight polyester crepe by Skinner.

But for fun – forget about trying to match that fashion fabric and find a contrasting lining that will add pzazz! Prints are super (make matching shirt or soft dress for an elegant costume). If wearing a print lined jacket over a different print dress offends you, look for some of the inoffensive and insignificant prints that really blend with anything. Stripes, dots, checks, and small two color prints are very versatile. Even in conservative menswear, linings are often loud but gorgeous – we saw a black gabardine Pierre Cardin business suit with a smashing RED PLAID lining!

NOTE: Susan has a beautiful silk scarf that she plans to recycle soon into a jacket lining. The scarf is large enough to line the jacket body and she will find a coordinating solid fabric for the sleeves.

## CUTTING THE LINING:

Linings in coats and jackets need a pleat for wiggle room and to keep the sleeves from tearing out with stress. If your pattern does not have a pleat, follow the method below:

1. Place lining back pattern on fold, slanting pattern so 1" is added at neckline tapering to nothing at bottom. Cut.

2. Stitch down 1 1/2" to anchor pleat at neckline.

Add 1" here

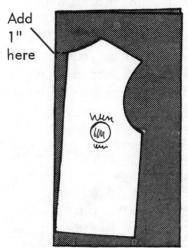

1 1/2"

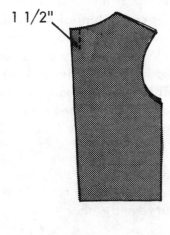

If you are using the Quick Lining method, cut the underarm of the bodice and sleeve 1/4" higher to allow lining to go up and over the sleeve underarm seam.

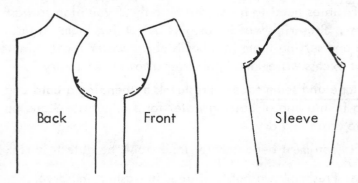

Back    Front    Sleeve

See page 104 for more on cutting a lining for a vented jacket.

# Preshrink !

Fashion Fabric-- If you plan to:
1.  Wash your tailored garment (heaven forbid!), preshrink in washer and dryer with detergent and same water temperature you plan to use when laundering.
2.  Dry clean your garment by the clean and press method, take your fabric to the drycleaners and have them pre-shrink it for you. This heavy steaming process will remove potential shrinkage caused by pressing.
3.  Use the "clean only" drycleaning method at a bulk cleaners, simply pre-steam your fabric on your cutting board (cover with a sheet if it is not a padded board). This will eliminate the possible shrinkage from pressing as you sew. Steam evenly and move the iron with the grain across the fabric. Do not move it on the bias.

NOTE: Pati and Susan use the "clean only" drycleaning method and do not preshrink fabric they plan to dryclean - in seven years there have been no shrinkage problems. Also, Pati found out recently that her drycleaner hangs things up immediately so all wrinkles hang out. If a cleaner allows the clothes to sit in a pile, wrinkles will be heat-set and virtually impossible to remove! Find a good bulk cleaners.

Interfacings: Hair canvas should be dampened and pressed until dry. Fusibles need to be preshrunk only if you plan to wash the garment. Preshrink woven fusibles by folding them into a neat square and setting them in a basin of hot water for 10 minutes. Pat out excess water and hang over a towel rod to dry.

Twill tape and seam tape: Preshrink by bending a card and setting it in a cup of boiling water for 5 minutes. Stand on edge to drain and dry.

NOTE: You must bend card or tape won't be able to shrink!

Linings: Preshrink washable linings in washer and dryer.

# Make Sure It Will Fit

### PATTERN SIZE

Buy the same size you would normally buy, because pattern companies automatically build in the extra ease needed for a coat or jacket to be worn over other clothes. Don't buy a larger pattern size for a heavy coating. Simply add "in-case" seams ("in-case" you need them!). Cut 1" seam allowances rather than 5/8" at shoulders, armholes, and sides of both the front and back pattern pieces. Then if the fabric takes up extra room as it goes around your body, you can let the seams out.

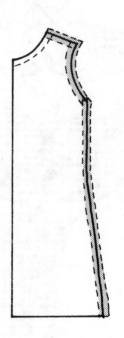

### EASE

Try on a jacket you currently have in your wardrobe to see how much ease you are accustomed to.

"QUICK PINCH TEST": Pinch the body and sleeve of a jacket to check the ease in a garment. If you pinch 2", that means that your jacket has 4" of ease at that spot. (You are pinching a double thickness of fabric.) Be sure you are pinching only one side, pulling all the fabric to that side.

| EASE CHART | | | | |
|---|---|---|---|---|
| | Bust | Hip | Sleeve (upper arm) | Back* |
| JACKET | 3-4" | 3-4" | 3-4" | 1-1 1/2" |
| COAT | 4-5" | 4-5" | 4-5 1/2" | 1-1 1/2" |

*6" below neck, armhole to armhole
(Reaching room!)

NOTE: See how the garment is shown on the pattern envelope. If a coat is shown worn over a jacket, then enough extra ease has been allowed for that purpose. If it is shown only over a lightweight dress, that is how it is meant to be worn and it will not have enough ease to be worn over anything bulkier. However, coats with lower and wider cut armholes, square armholes, or raglan sleeves can usually be worn over a blazer type jacket.

## TWO WAYS TO FIT A PATTERN

1. TRY THE PATTERN ON - (The easiest.) Trim excess tissue away and press pattern with warm dry iron. Pin in the darts and pin front and back seams together. Clip the armhole and neck curvature of the tissue pattern so it will lie flat. Try the pattern on over the same type of clothes you'll be wearing under the finished jacket. Pin the pattern center front and back to your center front and back -- to your clothes that is!

## CHECKPOINTS (Always work from top down so you won't miss anything.)

Shoulder seam – at center of shoulder.*

Shoulder width – 1/4"-1/2" beyond pivot bone in shoulder. (Jacket is worn over other clothes.)

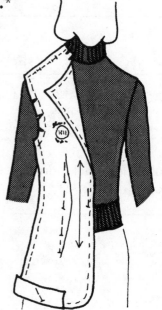

Grain line – perpendicular to floor at center back and front.

Side seams – hang straight. If your hips are larger than pattern, unpin so that pattern may fall freely. If side seams swing toward front, you have a sway back.

Bust darts – point to bust, but end 1" from point.

Armhole – fits smoothly. If the armhole gaps in the front, it means your bust is fuller than pattern; if the armhole gaps in the back, it means you have a rounded back.

Waist – should be at waist. (Waist is marked on pattern by dots at side seams.)

Length – Make sure hemline hits you at the most flattering part of your hip. This generally means below the fullest part of the fanny.

Sleeve – Try the sleeve pattern on after first checking the above. Pin large dot at top of sleeve to shoulder and pin underarm seam in place. Width is checked by pinching pattern at upper arm across from under arm to see amount of ease. Length--hemline should hit middle of wrist bone (or 1/2" below it for a coat).

*Shoulder seams in men's jackets and some women's angle toward back as a design line. Check line drawing of jacket back to see if shoulder is intentionally angled toward back.
44

2. <u>FLAT PATTERN MEASURE</u>-- If in doubt after trying on the
tissue pattern--double check with a tape measure. For example,
if the side seams of the pattern won't come together, measure
the pattern at the hip area and compare to your body hip measure-
ment to see how much you actually need to add to the sides.

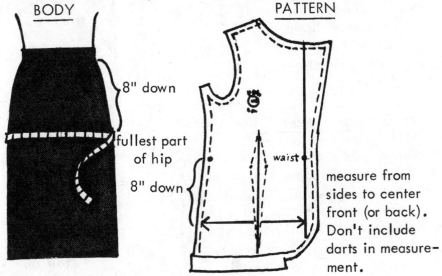

BODY                                    PATTERN

8" down

fullest part
of hip

8" down

waist

measure from
sides to center
front (or back).
Don't include
darts in measure-
ment.

If pattern front and back measure 20", (that is really 40" since
you are cutting double), and your hip is 36" at the fullest part,
then your pattern allows 4" ease which should be ample.

NOTE: Always flat pattern measure in the exact same place
you measured your body.

## FIVE TAILORING ALTERATIONS

Alter a jacket in the same manner you would alter any
other garment; however, the bulk of the fabric (in tailoring)
often hides minor problems. (The following are problems
you should <u>be sure</u> to correct.)

1. Extra width needed in
the hip area. Add to
sides of back and front
beginning at nothing
at armhole. If you need
2", divide 4 (number of
side seam allowances)
into 2" and add 1/2"
to each side when
you cut.

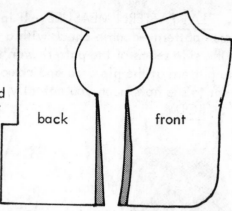

back    front

2. "Gaposis" of the roll line. There
are two things that you may do
if it gaps a small amount. Simply
shorten twill tape when sewing
to pull in the roll line so it hugs
your chest (page 55). If it gaps
a large amount, shorten roll
line by taking a tuck in pattern. (Be sure to make this
change on interfacing and
facing also.) This does not
change the "position" of the
roll line. It still begins and
ends at the same points.

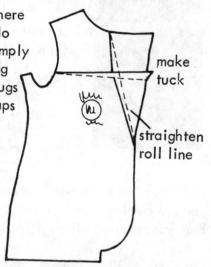

make
tuck

straighten
roll line

3. Sleeve too tight in upper arm. Measure arm at underarm
area. Alter sleeve as follows:

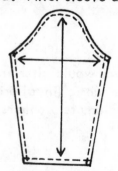

Measure pattern at
underarm area.

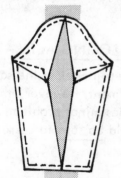

To add, cut on grain-
lines as shown and
spread desired amount.

46

4. Sway back or erect back causes side seams to swing forward and center back to swing toward side. This is why a vent won't stay closed on a finished garment. Pin pattern to center back. Take tuck until center back hangs straight. (Tuck may be made higher or lower or even 2 small tucks--see what seems to work best.) Straighten grainline by drawing line connecting top and bottom.

5. Bust Alterations--

Adding a dart --when you need to give more shape to a boxy jacket.

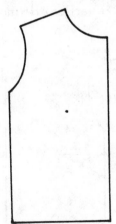

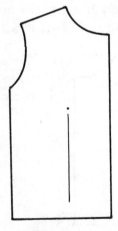

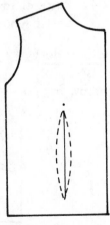

Find point of bust (apex) by trying on pattern.

Draw center line of dart from hip to apex, stopping 1" from apex.

Make dart as wide as you want it at waist.

47

Enlarge bustline--patterns are made for B bra cup size.  A C cup should have no problem, but a D cup may have to add extra room.  A gaping front armhole means enlarge bustline.

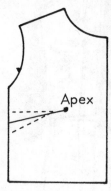 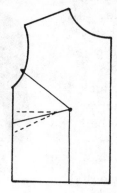 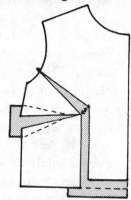

1. Draw a line through dart to apex.

2. Draw a line from waist to apex parallel to grain and then to arm- hole notch.

3. Cut along lines to but not through armhole. At arrow spread a minimum of 1/2" for C cup, 3/4" for D cup, 1 1/4" for DD cup.

4. Raise or lower dart if necessary and add a vertical fitting dart if you want a more fitted look.

Raise a dart
Raise point, redraw higher

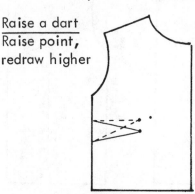

Lower a dart
Drop point, redraw lower

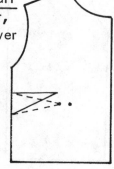

Shorten a dart

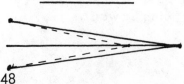

Lengthen a dart

<u>Add a bustline dart</u> – Many patterns have only a small vertical dart, which may not be enough if you are large in the bustline area (over a "C" cup). However, you can easily add a horizontal bustline dart.

1. Find apex. The easiest way is to try pattern on and mark point of bust with a pen.

2. Draw line (A) on your pattern where you would like a dart.

3. Draw line (B) from apex to armhole notch.

4. Draw line (C) vertically below apex to bottom of jacket.

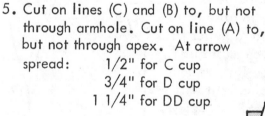

5. Cut on lines (C) and (B) to, but not through armhole. Cut on line (A) to, but not through apex. At arrow spread:     1/2" for C cup
    3/4" for D cup
    1 1/4" for DD cup

6. Insert tissue.

7. Side opening becomes dart. Raise or lower dart if necessary.

8. When you sew the bustline dart, your front and back side seams will again be the same length.

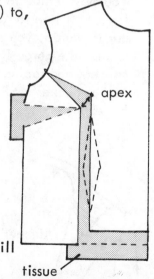

NOTE: Three added bonuses: your armhole will no longer gap; you will have more width across the bust; you will have more length going over your larger bust and your jacket will no longer hike up at bottom in the front.

49

## FITTING AS YOU SEW

1. After stitching darts, hold the front sections up to you to make sure the darts are where you want them.

2. After you have completed the front and back, pin sides and shoulders together. Try on to check length, width, and darts. Are the side seams hanging straight? Is the back vent closed? Take in or let out side seams if jacket doesn't fit in the hip area.

   NOTE: The neck must be staystitched so that it won't stretch (see page 62). If the fabric is stretchy or losely woven, you do not even hang it on a hanger until the collar is stitched on.

3. Pin sleeves together and slip on to "quick-check" width and length before hemming.

4. After collar is attached, check the roll line and gorge line. You may decide to raise or lower roll line for a better fit. But if you do, you must also change the gorge line on both garment and facing or it will pull or pucker as shown below. For example:

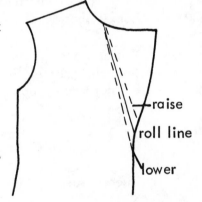

raise
roll line
lower

Lowering roll line makes excess fabric and puckers in gorge line — sew a deeper seam to correct.

Raising roll line causes gorge line stress — correct by taking a smaller seam allowance at gorge line.

50

# Cutting and Marking are Related

## CUTTING

1. Lining (see page 39).
2. Interfacing (see page 35).
3. Fashion fabric--things to check for <u>before</u> cutting:
   --Upper collar must be larger than under collar and facing must be larger than lapel (see page 56 for explanation of "turn-of-cloth"). The amount depends on the weight of your fabric. All patterns should allow at least 1/8". You may want to add more.

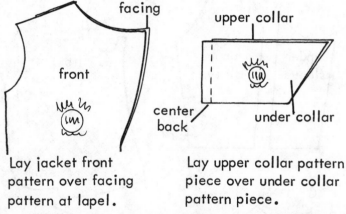

Lay jacket front pattern over facing pattern at lapel.

Lay upper collar pattern piece over under collar pattern piece.

--For a rolled collar that rolls smoothly, the under collar should be on the bias and cut in two pieces and have a center back seam. A one-piece all bias collar will have lengthwise grain (which is stronger) in opposite directions at collar points, and left and right may end up looking different.

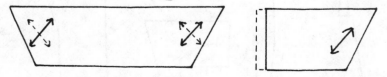

To correct: Cut pattern in half and add a center back seam allowance.

51

## MARKING

1. **SNIP MARK** when cutting for speed and greater accuracy. While cutting snip 1/4" into edge on all pieces – fashion fabric, underlining, interfacing and lining. Snip, don't cut, around notches. Snip mark all dots and matching points. Snip all the following points:

| | |
|---|---|
| notches | center front |
| shoulder dot | center back |
| side seam | collar point |
| hem fold | roll line |
| dart | vent fold |

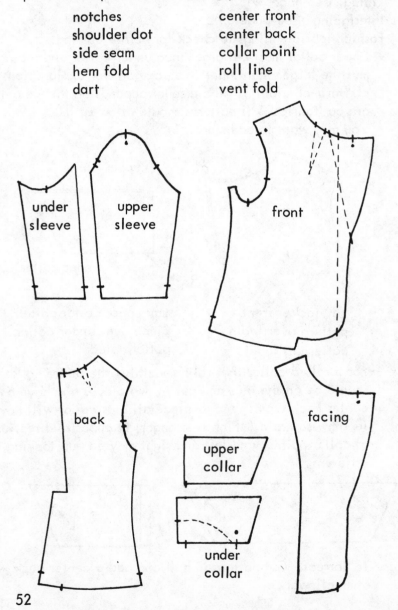

2.  Additional markings:

on underlining – use a tracing wheel and washable tracing paper to mark darts. It is not necessary to mark darts on fashion fabric.

on fashion fabric – try the tracing wheel. If it doesn't work, use the "pin-marking" method. Put pins through pattern dots. Remove pattern. Put pins in the bottom layer in the same place the pins came through. Now pin darts in place.

on interfacing – mark buttonholes, roll line and center front using lead or chalk pencil and ruler. Lay left and right interfacing on the table facing each other. Place the ruler between snips and draw a line with the lead pencil. When applying interfacing to fabric, pencil marks should be on top.

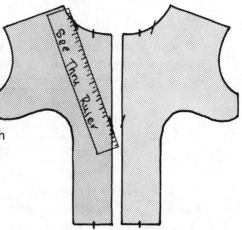

# Tailoring What's and Why's

These are some of the techniques that universally apply to tailored garments and the reasons why they are used ...

## 1. ELIMINATING BULK

Why:  There are usually more layers of fabric used in tailoring and they are often heavier than in a dress or skirt.

Interfacing – The interfacings in a tailored garment are generally heavier; therefore interfacing is not included in darts, neck, front, and underarm seams.  Trim seams away if your pattern has not done so.

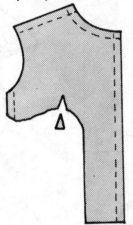 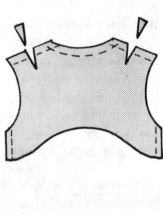

If your fabric is very bulky, you may also want to trim interfacing out of corners of a very pointed collar.

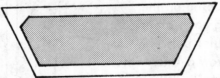

| | |
|---|---|
| Enclosed seams – due to the extra bulk of fabric and extra layers of shaping fabrics used in tailoring, it is necessary to trim and grade or bevel seams. | Trim seams to 1/4". Grade or layer inside seam to 1/8". |

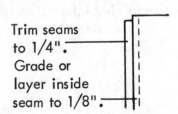

NOTE: You may trim and grade by "beveling." Simply slant scissors while trimming and one layer will automatically be narrower. Super on heavy coatings too – bevel seams one layer at a time.

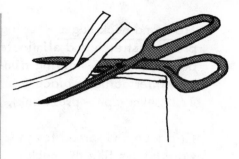

Darts – usually slashed and pressed open to spread the bulk evenly. (See page 27).

2. TAPING

Why : Tape is used to prevent stretch in garments that receive excessive wear such as a coat or jacket.

Roll line – which is on the bias. Tape keeps the roll line from stretching. Place 1/4" twill tape (preshrunk) next to the roll line and fell stitch in place.

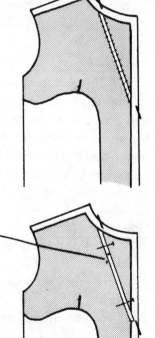

Go one step further and pull the tape tighter to prevent "gaposis" of the neckline and force the lapel to roll.

Pin tape flat. Make a pencil mark on the tape and mark on the interfacing the appropriate distance away. Pull tape until marks line up. Stitch in place easing evenly onto tape.

PULL the tape tighter:
by 1/4" for small bust
by 3/8" for medium bust
by 1/2" for full bust

Do both fronts at the same time so they look the same. 55

Front and neck edges – taping prevents stretch and eliminates bulk in seams by holding trimmed interfacing in place (use 1/2" seam tape – preshrunk).

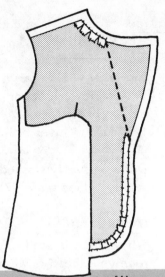

Clip tape and spread for inward curves like the neckline and clip tape and overlap on outward curves like the bottom of a jacket. Make sure uncut edge is next to seam line.

**NOTE:** If a fabric is stable or garment is not one you'll wear a lot, you may eliminate taping edges. Taping may be eliminated in the fusible method if the interfacing is included in seams.

3. ALLOWING FOR "TURN-OF-CLOTH" – in lapel and collar

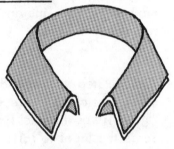

Why: It takes more fabric for the upper collar to roll over the under collar. Add to the outer edges of the upper collar if upper collar pattern piece is not already larger. (See page 51.)

How much to add:
1/8" for light-medium weight fabric
1/4" for medium-heavy weight fabric
3/8" for very heavy coatings

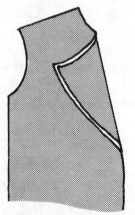

Also check lapel. Facing should be cut larger. See page 51 for how to cut larger if not allowed by pattern.

# Hand Stitches and their Alternatives

in "Custom" Method

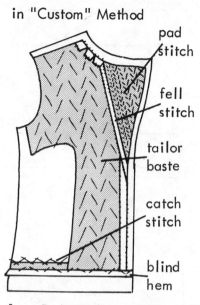

pad stitch

fell stitch

tailor baste

catch stitch

blind hem

in "Easiest" Method

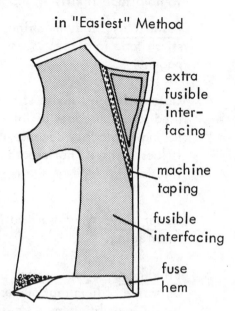

extra fusible inter- facing

machine taping

fusible interfacing

fuse hem

1. <u>Pad stitch</u> – small stitch that attaches interfacing to under collar and lapel. It accomplishes 3 things in one:
   - <u>adds body</u> – the closer and smaller the stitches, the more body.
   - <u>forces two layers to behave as one</u>
   - may create permanent roll by folding layers over hand while stitching.

   <u>Easier Ways:</u> by machine or by fusing.

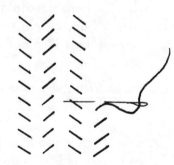

2. <u>Tailor basting</u> – large pad stitches used to hold large areas of interfacing in place. Use a size 10 sharp needle and catch only a fiber of fashion fabric so stitch won't show or catch only underlining.

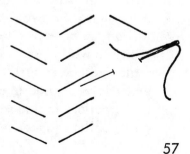

3. Fell stitch – a 3/8" long stitch used to hold tape tightly in place.

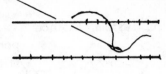

Easier Way: May machine stitch tape in place. (See page 69 ).

4. Catch stitch – a loose stitch used to catch edges of interfacing in place. Because it is loose, it will not create an interfacing ridge on the right side.

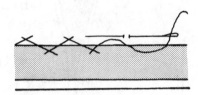

Easier Way: May use a fusible interfacing.

5. Blind hem – a loose stitch done on inside of hem that makes a truely invisible hem. Use a size 10 sharp needle and catch only a fiber of your fabric and make each stitch about 3/8" apart.

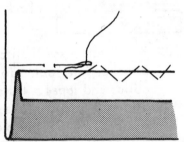

Easier Way: Fuse hem with fusible web.

6. Slip stitch – used for jump hem in lining and to attach pockets. When the thread is pulled tight, everything disappears.

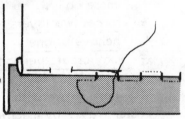

7. Stab stitch – a loose running stitch that joins two seams that fall on top of each other. Needle goes into well of seam on top at an angle and comes out of well on under layer. Used to attach upper collar/facing seam to under collar/jacket seam.

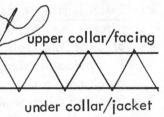

upper collar/facing

under collar/jacket

# Easy, Easier, Easiest. . .Which One?

The method you choose depends on your fabric and time. The following charts will help you select the best method. For example, if you have only 8 hours, the Time Chart below tells you that you must use the Easiest method. Then turn to the Fabric Chart and see which fabrics will work with that method. Note that linen works well with the Easiest method. OR, if you fell in love with a beautiful wool gabardine at your favorite fabric store, the Fabric Chart will tell you that Custom, Easy and Easier all work, but we prefer Easier, (it's speedy, yet gives quality results).

NOTE: You may use any method you wish for each jacket piece. If, however, you underline the front, you should also underline the back and sleeve for a consistent look.

Custom  - Primarily hand made - uses good quality hair canvas.

Easy    - Machine stitch hair canvas to an underlining - hand pad stitch lapels.

Easier  - Fuse a fusible hair canvas or other weight fusible interfacing to an underlining.

Easiest - Fuse a fusible hair canvas or other weight fusible interfacing directly to fashion fabric.

(Refer to page 10 for complete definitions)

## TIME CHART (in hours)

| TASK | CUSTOM | EASY | EASIER | EASIEST |
|------|--------|------|--------|---------|
| Cutting | 3 | 3 | 3 | 1 1/2 |
| Fronts | 10 | 6 | 4 | 1 |
| Back | 3 | 1 | 1 | 1/2 |
| Collar | 6 | 2 | 1 | 1/2 |
| Sleeves | 2 | 1 | 1 | 1 |
| Bound Buttonholes | 2 | 2 | 2 | |
| Lining | 4 | 2 | 2 | 2 |
| Finishing (Buttons, Buttonholes, Hems | 3 | 1 | 1 | 1 1/2 |
| | 33 | 18 | 15 | 8 |

# FABRIC CHART

KEY: X=it will work  XX=our preference–same quality but faster

| | CUSTOM | EASY/EASIER | EASIEST |
|---|---|---|---|
| **Wovens** | | | |
| Linen | X | X | XX |
| Synthetic Linen | X | X | XX |
| Linen-like | X | XX | |
| Wool Gabardine/Lt. Flannel | X | XX | |
| Wool Tweed/Heavy Flannel | X | X | XX |
| Wool Coatings | XX | | |
| Stretch-woven Polyesters | X | XX | X |
| Short-staple Polyesters | X | X | XX |
| Cotton Chintz | X | XX | |
| Heavy Cottons | X | X | XX |
| Denim | X | X | XX |
| Suit Weight Silk | X | XX | |
| **Napped Fabrics** | | | |
| Velveteen | X | XX | |
| Washable Velvet | X | XX | |
| Corduroy | X | XX | |
| Ultrasuede® | X | | XX |
| **Knits** | | | |
| Polyester Double Knit | X | X | XX |
| Wool Double Knit | X | X | XX |

NOTE : A sneaky way to use the Easiest method on almost any fabric. With some lightweight or flat surfaced fabrics, fusing to only part of the piece can create a ridge. Avoid this by choosing a pattern with a narrow front panel and fuse seam to seam as shown. Since fusibles can also be boardy, this limits that extra firmness to a smaller area.

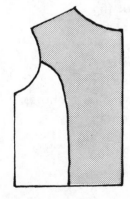

# The Pieces : Fronts
## CUSTOM TAILORED

Be sure to use a good hair canvas interfacing, like Armo P-1. Just ignore the underlining comments if you are not using one.

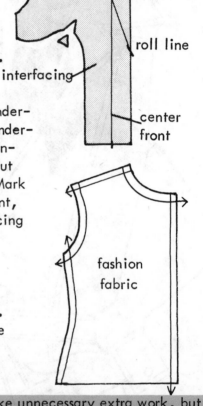

1. Cut interfacing, (see page 35) underlining and fashion fabric. Snip mark center front, roll line, and collar placement on all three (see page 52). Cut dart out of interfacing.

2. With an underlining, mark darts and buttonholes on underlining only. Without an underlining mark darts and buttonholes on fashion fabric. Cut darts out of interfacing. Mark entire roll line, center front, and buttonholes on interfacing only.

3. Directionally staystitch fashion fabric 1/2" from edge, all but bottom edge. The curved areas (bias) like the neck and armhole are a must!

NOTE: Staystitching seems like unnecessary extra work, but it's essential with loosely woven fabrics or a garment that will be handled a lot during construction. Staystitching is done to prevent stretching of cut edges. Stitch 1/2" from the edge as shown.

4. Place underlining on fashion fabric, lining up snips. Press together to remove any wrinkles.

5. Glue layers together on all <u>seam allowances</u> except bottom and lapel (leave loose to allow for "turn-of-cloth").

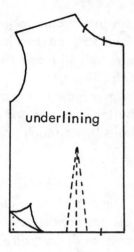

underlining

6. Sew darts. If underlining, place pins through darts to prevent slippage. Machine baste through center of dart to hold layers together. Stitch past point for a better hold and remove any stitches that show later. Then sew darts through all layers. Slash open and press flat (see page 27).

7. Make bound buttonholes now (see page 107).

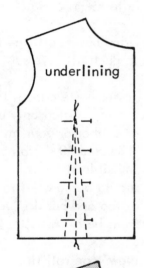

underlining

8. Prepare dart in interfacing. Cut a bias strip of lightweight lining fabric 1" wide and 1" longer than dart, and sew edges to it. Sew bias strip to one side. Pivot, bring dart edges together and sew down other side.

9. Pin interfacing to jacket front
(bias strip next to jacket). Be
sure roll line and center front
snips line up.
Trim a rectangle out where
buttonholes are and pull buttonhole lips through.

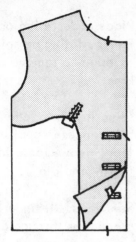

10. Trim 5/8" from interfacing in
all but armhole seams if your
pattern did not already eliminate them.

11. Hand baste roll line in place,
through all layers.

12. Tailor baste canvas to fashion
fabric. Catch only underlining
or a fiber of your fashion fabric.
(Use size 10 sharp needle for
invisible stitches.) Stitches
should be parallel to roll line
at top and parallel to center
front below roll line.

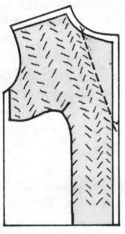

13. Now tape roll line with 1/4"
twill tape. Place twill tape
up against roll line, pull
1/4" to 1/2" tighter (see
page 55), and fell stitch
in place (see page 58).

NOTE: You may leave a 3" extension of twill tape at the top.
This will be attached to collar
roll line for extra strength (see
page 95 ).

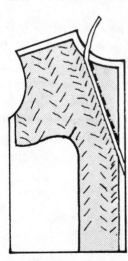

14. Shape lapel by rolling it over a wash cloth that has been rolled into a sausage shape, and steam it. Allow it to cool and dry before moving.

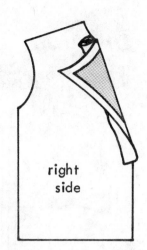

right side

15. Begin close to the roll line and pad lapel with stitches parallel to it, barely catching outside fabric. Hold lapel over your hand to create a permanent roll. Make stitches 1/8" in length and 1/8" apart for a distance of 3/4" from the roll line. Then they can be larger and 1/4" - 1/2" apart as you move to outside edge. Do not roll over hand as much as you approach outer edge or point will curl too much.

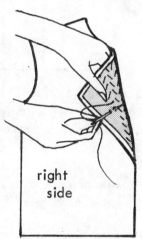

right side

16. Now tape neck and front edges with 1/2" seam tape (preshrunk). Place one edge against 5/8" seam line. Fell stitch both edges in place. May also tape the lapel if the fabric is quite stretchy.

17. Remove roll line basting.

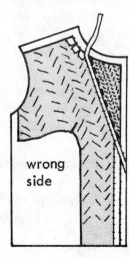

wrong side

center front

fold line

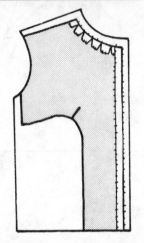

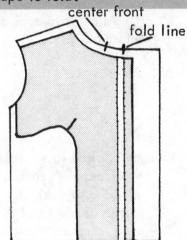

MODIFIED SPEED-TAPING METHOD: a way to avoid hand taping and still eliminate bulky hair canvas from seam allowances in a garment with a separate facing.

1. Cut a strip of lightweight lining (Poly SiBonne) 1" wide, same shape and grain as edge of front pattern piece.

2. After seam allowances have been trim- med from your interfacing, overlap lining 3/8" and glue-baste with Baste & Sew Glue Stik™.

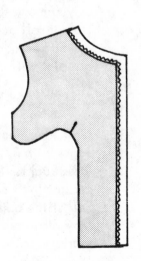

3. Stitch lining to edge of interfacing, lining side up, with one row of zig- zag or two rows of straight stitching.

4. Glue interfacing in place with Sobo.

5. Tailor baste interfacing, tape roll line. Continue as with Custom Front.

## FRONT PIECE: EASY

Must use an underlining. Be sure to use a hair canvas interfacing - either the best like Armo P-1 or Acro or a budget canvas like P-26.

1. Cut fashion fabric, under-lining, and interfacing. Snip mark center front, roll line, collar placement on all three.

2. Mark darts on underlining only. Cut darts out of interfacing. Mark entire roll line, center front, and buttonholes on interfacing only.

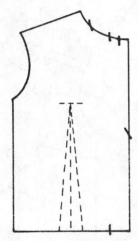

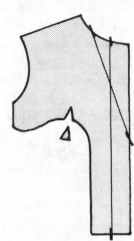

3. Place interfacing on underlining. Trim 5/8" from shoulder, neck, and front of interfacing if pattern is not already trimmed. Glue-baste interfacing to under-lining (dot over entire surface) with Baste & Sew Glue Stik™. This keeps interfacing from slipping while stitching. Let dry 5 minutes. (You may stitch through glue dots).

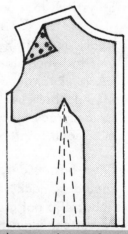

NOTE: If you are using a lightweight fabric and interfacing, you may leave interfacing in shoulder and underarm seams.

4. Machine stitch rows of stitching parallel to break line and
center front 1" apart, catching
interfacing to underlining.
If garment does not have a
lapel, make all rows parallel
to center front. Zig-zag or
straight stitch around dart
1/16" from cut edge.

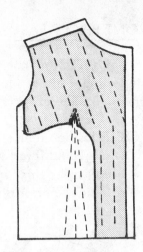

5. Stitch 1/2" seam tape to neck
and front edges of interfacing
and underlining, using straight
or zig-zag machine stitches on
both edges. May glue-baste
seam tape in place first with
Baste & Sew Glue Stik.

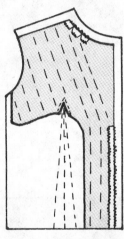

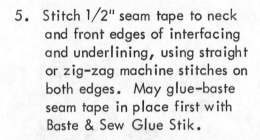

NOTE: Taping is optional with this
method since underlining will act
as a stabilizer. However, coats that
get lots of wear and loosely
woven woolens should be taped.

6. Staystitch fashion fabric.

7. Apply underlining/interfacing
unit to wrong side of fashion
fabric matching all snip marks.
May double check both fronts
for accuracy by placing pattern
over each front.

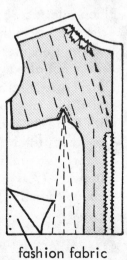

8. Glue-baste sides, armhole,
shoulder, neck, and front with
Sobo. Do not glue-baste lapel
or bottom edges together. Hand
baste through all layers on roll
line.

fashion fabric

9.  Sew darts through underlining
    and fashion fabric all in one.
    Do not catch interfacing.
    Slash open and press. (See
    page 27).

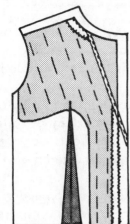

10. Tape roll line. Pull tighter
    by 1/4" - 1/2" (See page 55)
    and straight stitch or zig-zag
    in place.

NOTE: CHEAT! When
machine taping the roll
line, stitch the last two
inches at the bottom by
hand so your machine
stitches won't show on
the outside.

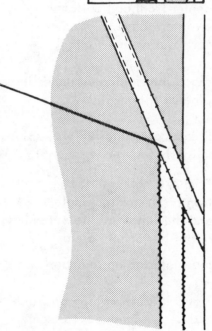

11. Roll lapel over wash cloth and steam into shape.
    (See page 65.)

12. Hand pad lapels over your hand. (See page 65.)

13. To eliminate bulk, trim away a rectangle 1/4" wide and
    the length of the buttonholes in the area where buttonholes
    will be made. Make bound buttonholes.

## FRONT PIECE : EASIER

You must use an underlining, but you may use any fusible interfacing depending on how much body is needed. Fusible Acro is the only fusible hair canvas and wears extremely well.

1. Cut fashion fabric, underlining and interfacing. Snip mark center front, collar placement and roll line on all three.

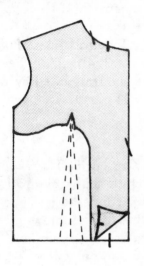

2. Mark darts on underlining only. Mark entire roll line, center front and buttonholes on interfacing only. Cut darts out of interfacing.

3. Place interfacing on underlining. Line up snip marks.

4. Steam baste interfacing in place (slightly fuse--one second).

5. Trim 5/8" off interfacing neck and fronts. Trim a rectangle 1/4" wide and the length of the buttonhole out of buttonhole area.

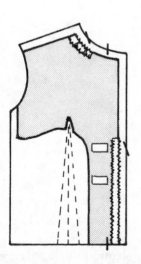

6. Fuse interfacing to underlining.

7. Place 1/2" seam tape on front and neck edges next to seam line. Glue-baste tape in place with Baste & Sew Glue Stik™, clipping tape where necessary (see page 56). Straight stitch or zig-zag both edges of tape in place.

NOTE: Taping is optional here since underlining acts as a stabilizer. However, coats that get lots of wear should be taped.

8. Place underlining/interfacing unit on fashion fabric, lining up snips. Lay pattern on top of each front to check.

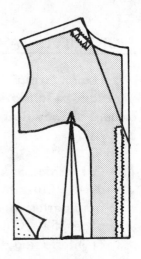

9. Glue-baste all but lapel and bottom edges with Sobo.

10. Directionally staystitch all but bottom and lapel.

11. Hand or machine baste through roll line bottom to top.

NOTE: For a princess style front, trim and fuse interfacing to underlining before stitching as shown.

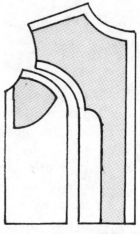

12. Sew darts through underlining and fashion fabric (see page 63). Slash and press open.

13. Tape roll line. Pin 1/4" twill tape next to roll line - pull tighter by 1/4"- 1/2" (see page 55) and zig-zag or straight stitch in place. Hand stitch last 2" so stitching line won't show on the outside. (See page 69).

14. Press lapel over rolled up wash cloth to shape it. No need to pad-stitch as fusible gives body - underlining and tape help it roll.

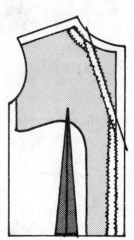

15. Glue-baste (with Sobo) underlining to fashion fabric seam allowances in lapel area while lapel is still rolled over wash cloth. Allowing for "turn-of-cloth" helps create roll.

16. Make bound buttonholes.

## FRONT PIECE: EASIEST

Use any weight fusible interfacing and fuse directly to your fashion fabric. Be sure to do a test sample. Check for amount of body fusible interfacing gives, and for a ridge on outside.

1. Cut fashion fabric. Mark darts. Cut interfacing, using front pattern piece. (See page 35). Cut dart out of interfacing.

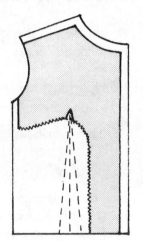

NOTE: Pink inside edge of interfacing to make it more invisible.

2. Trim away 1/2" of interfacing seam allowances, as shown, to reduce bulk.

3. Fuse interfacing to fashion fabric following interfacing manufacturers instructions.

extra piece of interfacing

NOTE: For extra body, you may steam baste an extra piece of interfacing to lapel under interfacing. Make it 1/4" smaller on outside edges and place against roll line.

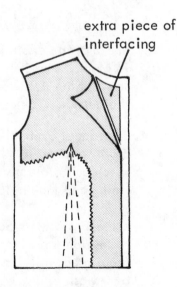

4. Machine tape roll line. (See page 71).

5. Sew darts.

6. Do bound buttonholes now, or machine buttonholes after jacket is finished.

## ALTERNATE FUSING METHODS

(Trim 1/2" off seam allowances of interfacing.)

1. <u>Fuse to facing and
   and lapel only</u>...
   a quick ready-to
   wear method that is
   best for jackets with
   machine buttonholes.

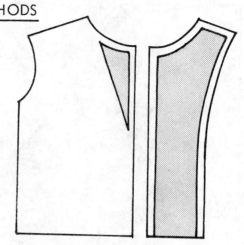

2. <u>Princess line.</u>

   a. Fuse chest, arm-
      hole and front
      edge. Trim 1/2"
      off interfacing
      except in arm-
      hole area.

   b. Fuse entire front
      if method "a"
      leaves a ridge at
      interfacing edge.

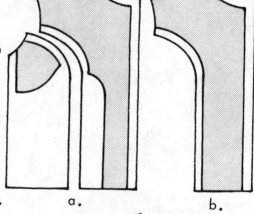

a.

b.

3. <u>Vertical princess line
   with narrow front lapel</u>...
   fuse to entire front. Trim
   1/2" off seam allowances
   of interfacing except in
   armhole.

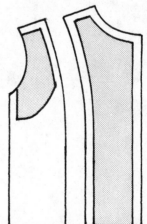

# The Pieces : Backs

General comments: A "back stay" or back interfacing is abso-
lutely necessary for a good looking, durable garment – remember
your jacket spends 90% of its life on a hanger.  The back stay
is best cut in one piece from armhole to armhole in order to
absorb "reaching stress".  If a pattern piece is not included for
a back stay, cut one according to instructions on page 35.

 If your back stay is cut from a hair canvas, it is best to
trim away seam allowances.  However, if your fabric and back
stay are not bulky, include them in the seam allowance – this
eliminates hand catching seams to interfacing later.

NOTE:  Some people cut a back stay on the bias for softness,
but stability is sacrificed...this is fine for a stable polyester
double knit but not recommended for other fabrics.

BACK PIECE:  CUSTOM  (with or without an underlining)

 Since there is such a small amount of hand stitching on the
back anyway, we often prefer to use the Custom method on all
backs.  Veriform Durable Press is a good fabric for a back stay;
for more shape, use a hair canvas.

1.  Cut fashion fabric, interfacing
    and underlining.

2.  Mark darts on underlining and
    interfacing (on fashion fabric
    if no underlining is used).

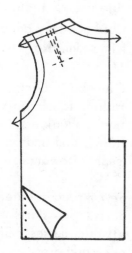

3.  Glue-baste underlining to
    fashion fabric.  Stay stitch
    each piece directionally
    where necessary.

4.  Sew line of stitching through
    center of darts, stitch through
    both layers.  Slash open and press.

75

5. Sew center back seam and press open.

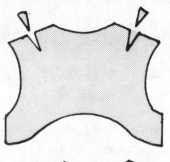

6. Cut darts out of interfacing. Sew darts as on page 63.

7. Place interfacing on back. Trim 5/8" off neck, shoulder, and underarm seams.

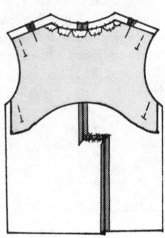

8. Using 1/2" seam tape, tape neck edge by hand. Use fell stitch (see page 58). Leave shoulders and sides of interfacing free as they will be caught in place later--simply pin to hold now.

## AN ALTERNATE CUSTOM METHOD

This method may be used with lighter weight fabrics to save time---it is FASTER because neckline taping is eliminated. Use a lighter wieght back stay fabric such as Veriform Durable Press. Include it in all seams and darts.

1. Cut back stay according to instructions on page 35. Do not trim seam allowances off. Mark darts on back stay only.

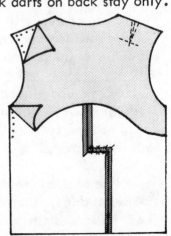

2. Glue-baste back stay to fashion fabric unit on neck, shoulders, armholes, and underarm seam allowances.

3. Sew through center of darts. Sew darts through all thicknesses. Slash open and press.

## BACK PIECE: EASY/EASIER

These methods apply to an <u>underlined</u> jacket with a one-piece back <u>without a vent</u>. You may use the same interfacings as suggested in Custom or any medium to heavyweight fusible. Machine stitch (or fuse) the interfacing to the underlining, then underline the back unit.

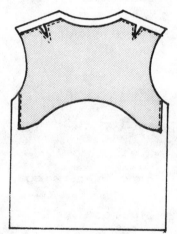

1. Mark darts on underlining. Cut dart out of interfacing.

2. Place interfacing on underlining. Trim 5/8" seam allowances off neck, shoulder, and underarm if pattern did not eliminate them.

3. <u>EASY</u> - Glue-baste interfacing to armhole seam allowances with Baste & Sew Glue Stik™. Machine stitch 1/16" from edge of interfacing at dart, shoulder, and underarm to hold in place.

   <u>EASIER</u> - Use fusible interfacing and fuse to underlining.

4. Machine stitch 1/2" seam tape to neck edge clipping as on page 56.

5. Glue-baste interfacing/underlining unit to fashion fabric with Sobo glue.

## BACK PIECE: EASIEST

Fusing directly to your fashion fabric across the back almost always leaves a ridge on the outside. We really would only suggest it on a heavy polyester double knit or a fabric with lots of body or texture to hide the fusible. Always do a test sample first to see if the fusible shows. Use a light or medium weight fusible and fuse to a one or two piece back as follows:

1. Cut back stay. Cut out darts. Trim 1/2" off neck, shoulders, and underarms. On a two piece back, also trim 1/2" off center back seam.

2. Fuse interfacing to back.

NOTE: To prevent ridge, pink bottom edge of interfacing.

3. Staystitch neck edge.

4. Stitch darts.

5. Sew center back seam.

One piece back

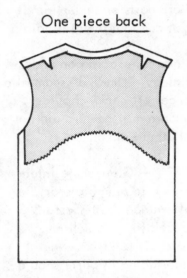

Two piece back

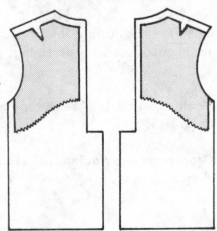

78

## Interfacing a vent

Interface left vent for wrinkle resistance and to prevent stretching since it is the one that is on the outside. The right vent is left uninterfaced to reduce bulk. Also see hem interfacing techniques on page 98.

Custom method - interfacing is included in fold for a firm, crisp edge. Place interfacing 1/2" past vent fold and hem fold on garment side, and catch stitch interfacing in place. Use Veriform Durable Press or a hair canvas.

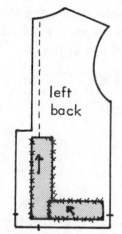

snip hemline

Easiest method - fuse interfacing to fold line of vent and hem. Trim 1/2" off outer edges.

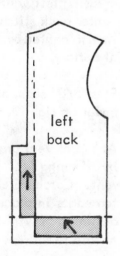

hem fold

NOTE: Hem interfacing is on the bias so that it will go around your body softly.

## BACK VENT

### Sewing a vent

1. Sew center back seam to dot. Press open.

2. Snip right back seam allowance to center of last stitch.

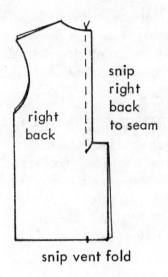

snip vent fold

3. Press toward left back, creasing left vent from center back stitching line to center back snips at bottom.

4. Press 5/8" seam allowance under on right vent.

5. At top of vent grade edges by trimming 1/4" off right vent. Catch stitch both top edges in place to underlining or with fine needle to fashion fabric.

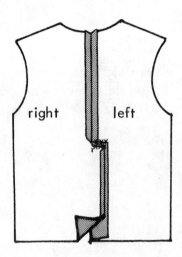

fold vent at snip

## Mitering a vent

This is a super clean finish for the bottom of the left vent. Easy to do, too!

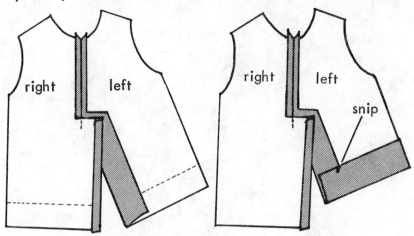

1. Fold left back vent from center back snip at bottom to center back seam line. Press.

2. Fold up hem allowance and snip intersection where edges meet.

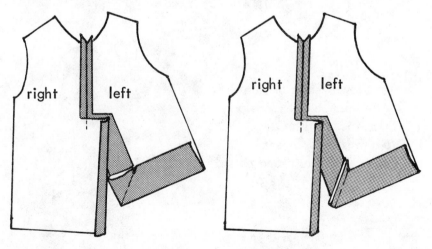

3. Unfold and line up snips.

4. Trim from snip to corner leaving 1/4" seam allowances.

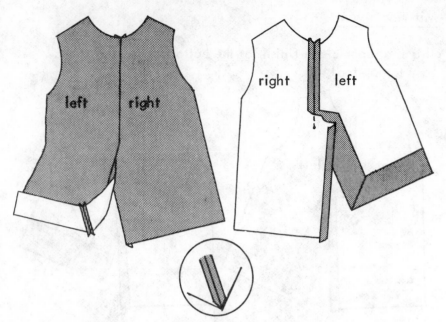

5. Turn right sides together and stitch 1/4" seam.

6. Diagonally trim seam at corner to eliminate bulk. Turn and press.

7. Turn lower edge of right back vent to outside along hem line. Stitch edges together on 5/8" seam line. Trim, turn and press.

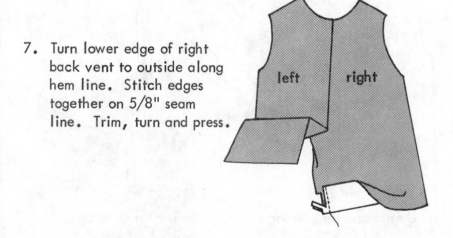

# The Pieces : Collars

<u>Upper Collar</u> - Be sure to read about turn-of-cloth before cutting collars, page 56.  Upper collar may be under-lined to cushion outer seam allowances.

1. Press the two layers together.

underlining

2. Glue baste - dot glue on seam allowances and pat together.

SOBO

underlining

<u>Under Collar</u> - Follow cutting instructions on page 51.

1. Cut under collar and interfacing on bias.  Mark roll line with snips on fashion fabric and with pencil or tracing wheel on interfacing.

fall

snip

roll line

stand

2. Sew center back seam of under collar and press open.  Trim to 1/4"

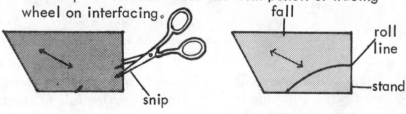

3. Trim 5/8" off interfacing at center back and outside edges. Slip interfacing under center back seam allowance and catch stitch seam allowance to interfacing.  Catch stitch outer edges of interfacing to collar.

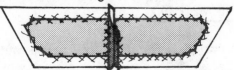

4. Stitch center back seam allowances flat 1/8" from well of
seam. This adds extra body
to center back.

5. Hand baste on roll
line barely catching
outer fabric.

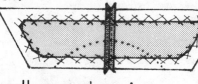

6. Shape under collar around pressing
ham by pinning collar to ham and
steaming. Let collar cool and dry
before moving.

7. Now is the time for "TV-time" stitches. Hand pad stitch
stand of collar with tiny stitches in an up and down direction, starting at center back and working toward outside
edges. Pad stitch fall of collar parallel to roll line starting
at center back on both sides. Use tiny stitches near roll
line and larger ones as you move torward outer edges.

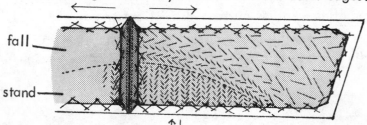

fall

stand

8. Curve collar over your
hand while stitching to
create a curve at roll
line.

9. Curve collar over your hand
while stitching fall to create
a permanent curve around
your neck.

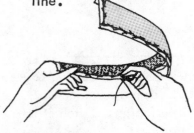

EASY MACHINE METHOD
Under collar -
1. Follow instructions 1 through 6 in Custom Method.

2. Machine padstitch vertically in stand and horizonatally in fall of collar using 12 stitches per inch. (You may use the "three-step" zig-zag on the fall of the collar.)

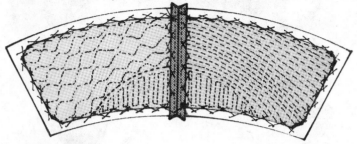

## EASIEST FUSIBLE METHOD

<u>Upper Collar</u> - Either glue or baste underlining as in custom collar, or fuse a lightweight fusible to upper collar.  Trim 1/2" from outside edges.

<u>Under Collar</u>
1. Trim 1/2" off all edges of fusible interfacing.  Fuse to each half of under collar.  Snip roll line on Fashion Fabric and trace or pencil mark roll line on interfacing.

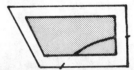 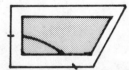

NOTE: If using a "woven" fusible, cut interfacing on bias. If using a "nonwoven" fusible, cut interfacing with <u>stretch</u> going around neck.

2. For extra body in the stand area, cut another piece of interfacing the shape of the stand.  Trim 1/2" off lower edge.  Fuse it to stand below roll line after center back seam is sewn.

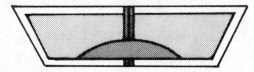

3. Pin to pressing ham and steam roll line as in Custom Method.

# The Pieces : Sleeves

The "Easiest" sleeve is a one piece sleeve, but the two-piece vented sleeve as shown below is always popular. We hear screams from the sewing room from those trying to get a professional finish on the lower edge of the vent.
Our answer – try the same mitering technique we showed you for the back vent on page 81.

## Cutting and Marking

1. If there is a vent extension below hem edge, cut it off pattern if you are planning to use the mitered vent technique.

2. Add a horizontal extension the same width as hem to side of sleeve from dot out. Begin 5/8" above dot.

3. Snip notches and underarm dots in under sleeve and shoulder dot at top of upper sleeve. Also snip hem folds.

under sleeve

upper sleeve

add here

snip away

NOTE: Did you know that one notch always means FRONT of sleeve and two notches always mean BACK of sleeve?

## Sew Sleeve

Glue underlining (if using one) in place on all but hem edges
before sewing sleeve.

1. Sew side front seam.
   Press open.

2. Machine baste 2 rows across
   top of sleeve, notch to
   notch one on 5/8" line and
   one 1/4" away. (See "Setting in a Sleeve," page 91.)

3. Trim seam in hem area
   to 1/4".

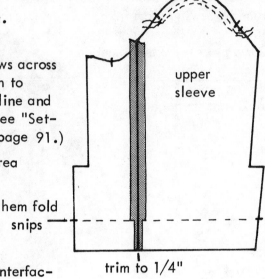

upper
sleeve

hem fold
snips

trim to 1/4"

## Prepare Hem

1. Cut a bias strip of interfacing (Acro or Veriform Durable
   Press) 1" wider than hem width.

2. Place interfacing 1/2"
   below fold line of sleeve.
   Trim 5/8" off outer edges.

3. Press hem up and crease
   from snip to snip.

4. Do a long running stitch
   along fold to hold interfacing to hem crease.

5. Catch-stitch top and bottom
   of interfacing to underlining
   or fashion fabric.

6. Finish bottom of sleeve by
   zig-zagging if necessary.

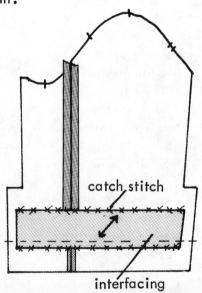

catch stitch

interfacing

NOTE: For "Easiest" method, fuse interfacing to foldline on
hem allowance.

## Mitered Vent

The upper vent on the upper sleeve (double-notched side) may be mitered for a clean finish. Under vent is not mitered.

1. Fold on vent fold line, then fold hem up. Snip corner where they come together.

2. Pull fold out and line up snips. Trim to 1/4" from snips to corner (see page 81).

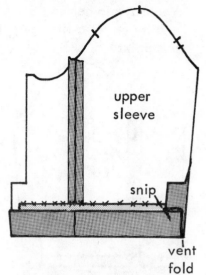

upper sleeve

snip

vent fold

3. Turn vent to right side and stitch 1/4" seam from snips to corner. Slash across corner to eliminate bulk and press seam open (see page 82).

4. Fold hem up on underlap side at hem snip, right sides together, and stitch 1/4" seam. Trim seam, slash across corner.

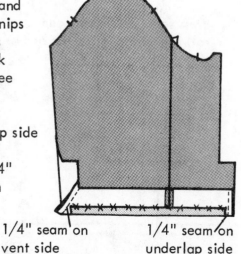

1/4" seam on vent side

1/4" seam on underlap side

5. Turn to inside and press.

### Finish Sleeve

1. You can hem sleeves flat before sewing second seam! You may pin hem and seam and try on for a fitting at this point.

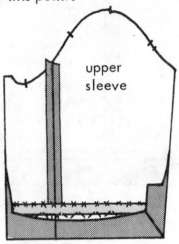

2. Sew sleeve seam to dot. Clip underlap side to dot.

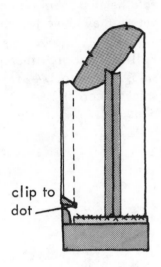

clip to dot

3. Press seam open over seam roll and catch stitch top and sides of vents in place.

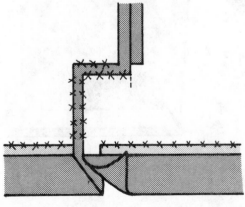

4. Sew 2 to 4 buttons on through both layers. (Small, closely spaced buttons are super!)

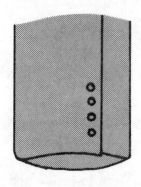

NOTE: Some patterns say to put bound or machine buttonholes in vent--ugh! Unnecessary!

90

## Setting in a Sleeve - Method I

1. Machine baste two rows of stitching from notch to notch over the sleeve cap. Place one row at 3/8" from the edge and the other at 5/8". Pull on the 3/8" stitching only, forming the cap. (5/8" line acts only as a final stitching guide.) Set in sleeve by pinning in place and machine basting. Try on for fit and permanent stitch again on 5/8" and 1/4" edge.

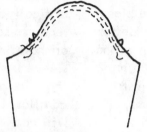

2. Trim seam under arm to 1/4" from notch to notch.

3. Always press sleeve cap from the inside. Do not top-press the cap.

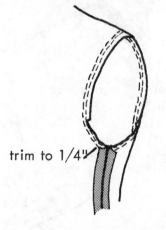

trim to 1/4"

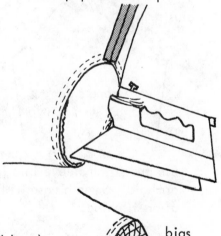

4. Bias strips (1 1/2" wide, 12" long) of lambswool, Tri-Shape, or Pellon Fleece stitched to the seam line of the sleeve cap from notch to notch over the sleeve cap will fill out the cap and give it the desired shape.

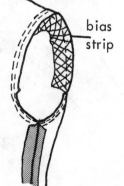

bias strip

## Setting in a Sleeve--Method II

The sound of the term "setting in a sleeve" often makes the strongest soul quake--and it shouldn't. Read on to find out about a great new way to get a PUCKER FREE set-in sleeve! We first discovered it as a sure-fire way to set in a sleeve in Ultrasuede.®

1. Purchase 3/8 yd. of Stacy's Tri-Shape interfacing. Cut one bias strip 12" long and 1 1/2" wide for each sleeve. Place strip on wrong side of sleeve cap, lining up top edges. Sew to sleeve cap just inside the 5/8" stitching line, stretching bias to fullest while stitching.

2. Sleeve cap is automatically eased and ready to sew into armhole. Even if sleeve is still a bit large for armhole, additional fullness will ease in smoothly. Press from inside cap to shrink in ease.

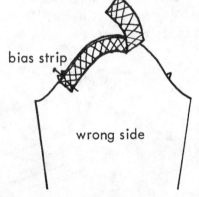

bias strip

wrong side

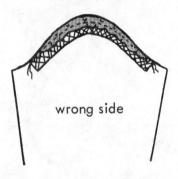

wrong side

3. Pin and stitch sleeve into jacket armhole. Smooth ease with fingers after stitching.

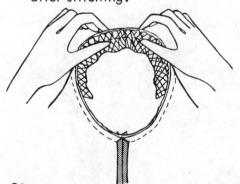

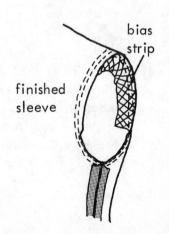

bias strip

finished sleeve

# Putting All The Pieces Together

It is best to follow general pattern instructions when sewing a jacket or coat together; however, there are some important points to be aware of that won't be found in a pattern.

1. <u>Sew front to back at shoulder and sides.</u>  Catch stitch shoulder and side seams to interfacing.

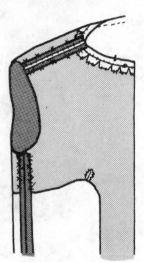

2. <u>Tape shoulders</u> (unless interfacing is included in seam for stability as in Easiest method).  Center 1/2" seam tape over shoulder seam and fell stitch in place.

3. <u>Attach under collar to garment.</u>

   - Sew under collar to garment from dot to dot.

   - Press seam open over long curve on the June Tailor board.  (See page 24 ).

   - Trim seam allowances to 1/4" and catch stitch in place.

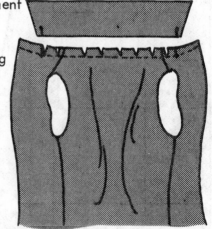

NOTE: If a 3" extension was left on the roll line twill tape (page 64), fell stitch it to collar (below roll line).

4. <u>Hem garment</u> (see page 98).

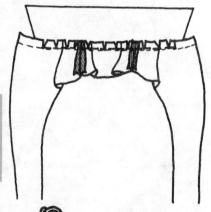

5. <u>Sew upper collar to facings.</u> between large dots. Press seam open over long curve on June Tailor board. Trim seam allowances to 3/8" and catch stitch in place.

NOTE: Attach lining unit to upper collar/facing unit now if using the Quick Lining method. (see page 101).

6. <u>Check the way the pieces fit together.</u> Place upper collar/ facing unit on under collar/garment, wrong sides together. Hang on a hanger to see if if the lapels and collars fall correctly Pin through gorge lines to hold them in place. Make sure facing is the same length as jacket bottom. If not, trim until even.

7. <u>Pin upper collar/facing unit to under collar/garment unit</u> right sides together.

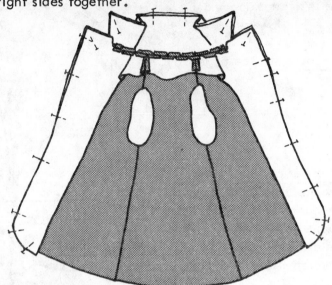

NOTE: Make a "Tailor's Blister" in order to get rid of excess fabric in upper collar and upper lapel points which have been cut larger to allow for "turn of the cloth". Pin a small tuck about 1/2" from point. Remove pin after outer seams have been stitched.

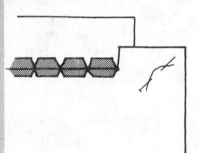

8. <u>Stitch outer edges together.</u> Use 20 stitches per inch at all corners and curves where close trimming is required.

Move seam allowances out of way. Stitch from dot to center back of collar on each side.

Move all seam allowances toward collar. Stitch from dot to bottom of jacket.

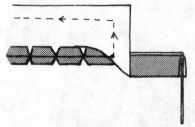

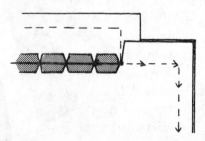

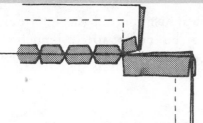 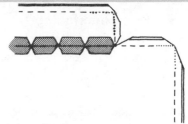

9. Clip to seam line at bottom of roll line so lapel will roll better. Press all seams open over proper pressing equipment.

10. Turn and press.

NOTE: Soap your seams - a neat trick to give outside edges a firm crease. Rub a bar of Ivory soap between seam allowances before pressing. (Avoid colored, perfumed, or deodorant soaps!)

11. Stabstitch collar seams together through wells of upper and under collar seams. (See page 58.)

CHEAT - If the upper collar is not large enough to go over under collar so that outer seams won't show (not enough "turn-of-cloth" allowance) - slip this upper collar/facing neck seam until upper collar is large enough. Anchor at that point instead of centering over under collar/garment seam.

12. Hem jacket and sleeve lining with jump hem.

13. If Quick-Lining - hand slip stitch front armhole of lining to front armhole seam of jacket to hold lapels in place.

14. Set in sleeves and pad caps with lambswool (see page 91).

15. Attach shoulder shapes (page 124) and lining (page 99).

# Hems

1. Press up hem in fashion fabric and crease fold line (leave 1/2" of front interfacing in hem fold line unless too bulky).

2. Cut a strip of bias interfacing (lightweight canvas or Veriform Durable Press) 1" wider than hem allowance.

3. Place interfacing 1/2" beyond hem fold. Baste interfacing to fashion fabric at fold line, but do not stitch through to outside. Lap 1/4" over front interfacing, catch stitch hem interfacing in place.

4. Grade facing seam to 1/4" in hem area to reduce bulk.

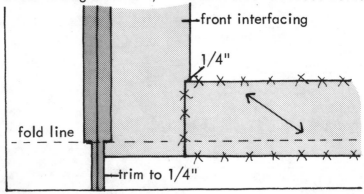

front interfacing

1/4"

fold line

trim to 1/4"

5. Turn up hem. Trim as shown to eliminate bulk. Using catch stitch, hem to facing and front interfacing. Hem rest of jacket with blind hem stitch.

NOTE: If hem is curved, machine baste 1/4" from edge and ease hem to fit garment. Zig-zag edge of hem if fabric is very ravely.

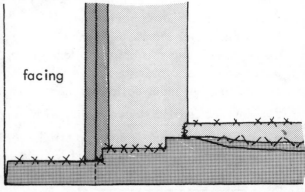

facing

98

# Lining...Three Methods

1. Custom – done almost entirely by hand and is helpful with heavy fabric or a heavy lining that is difficult to handle. This method gives the best fit in a lining.
2. Quick Lining – a super-fast machine method that gives great results!
3. Combination method – gives a fast machine-stitched lining but yet a custom fit in the shoulder area. Just follow Quick Lining steps but attach the lining sleeve to the garment by hand.

## LINING – CUSTOM METHOD

1. Cut lining as shown on page 39.
2. Stitch darts and back seam, press pleat to one side and tack with cross stitches below neckline.

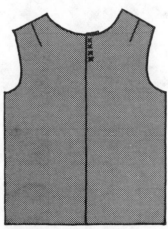

3. Stitch all side seams, press open. Staystitch at 1/2", press under front, shoulder and neck seam allowances, clip and notch where necessary.

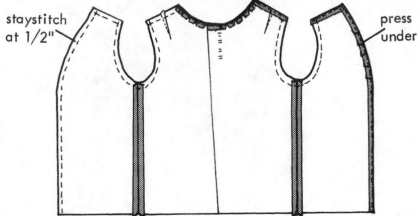

staystitch at 1/2"

press under

4. Stitch sleeve seam, press open. Easestitch sleeve cap, staystitch underarm area.
5. Pin lining into body of garment by keying underarm seams and shoulder seams.
6. Slipstitch fronts, neckline, shoulders. Baste armhole edges together, trim lining to match garment armhole.

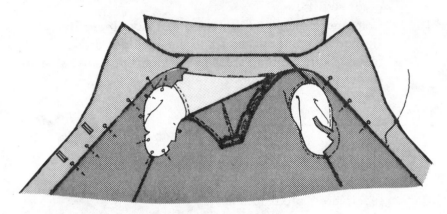

7. Slip lining over sleeve cap, match notches and sleeve top dot. Pull ease stitching threads until lining fits sleeve comfortably. Clip or trim underarm area as needed. Slip stitch lining sleeve cap in place.

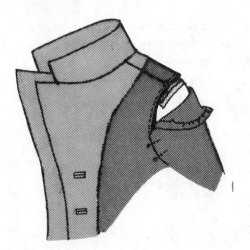

# "QUICK LINING" METHOD

1. Assemble all garment pieces – back, front, and sleeves. Stitch under collar to body of garment. Garment bottom and sleeves should be hemmed.

2. Assemble all lining pieces – back, front, and sleeves.

3. Assemble facing unit, attach upper collar to staystitched and clipped neckline.

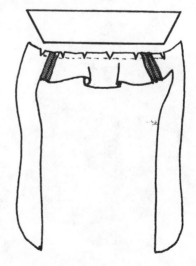

4. Sew the facing/upper collar unit to lining using 5/8" seam. Press toward lining.

5. Place collars right sides together. Pin remaining front edges together. Stitch outside edges together. Trim, layer, clip, notch, and slash seams where necessary. Turn garment right side out.

6. Press finished garment Hand "jump hem" lining sleeves and bottom as on page 103.

NOTE: Hand tack lining at front of armhole to prevent facing from creeping at front edge.

## HEMMING THE LINING

The truth about lining hems:

1. Let them "move" -- make a "jump" hem as illustrated below and they will never pull out.
2. Always (and we don't often use this word) cut lining to the length of the hemmed finished garment. Most patterns are already cut this way. Linings will now be shorter than the garment and will not show.

### "Jump" hem at bottom of jacket

1. Turn lining hem under until raw edge matches top edge of garment hem.
2. Pin in place about 1" from bottom fold of lining.
3. Lift hem fold and slipstitch , catching only the hem allowance of the lining and not the lining itself.

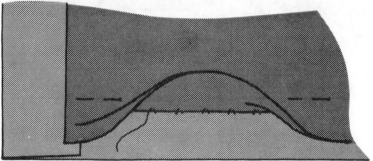

### "Jump" hem in a sleeve

1. Turn back the bottom edge of sleeve. (It's easier to handle that way since the sleeve is such a small cylinder).
2. Turn lining hem edge under 5/8" and match raw edge to top of sleeve hem.
3. Slip stitch in place. A "jump" will automatically be created.

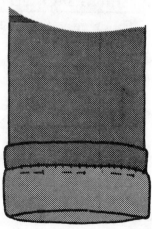

# THE GOOF-PROOF BACK VENT IN A LINING

Have you ever had problems figuring out which side of the lining in the vent area to cut away?  This one is Goof-Proof!

NOTE:  Left and right refer to when the jacket is on your back. A vent is like a lapped zipper – it laps left over right.

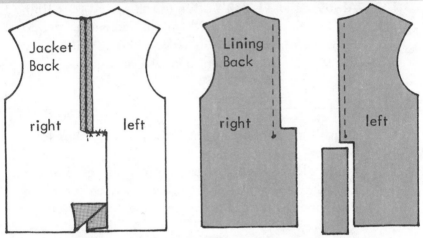

1.  Cut lining
2.  Mark cut-away section (as on pattern) with tracing paper on both back pieces.  Do not cut anything out of vent area yet.
3.  Sew center back seam to large dot.
4.  Lay lining on jacket wrong sides together.  Cut away left back.

## FINISHING BACK VENT

For an easy-to-do, flat look, even designers have decided machine topstitching the edges of the under vent is best.

1.  Assemble lining as on page 99.
2.  Save work – machine stitch right vent and lining edges together (Calvin Klein does!). (Hand slip stitch top of vent and left side.)

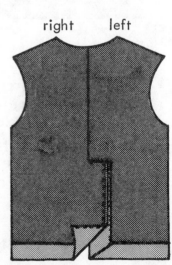

# WHAT TO DO WITH AN "UNLINED" JACKET

1. Easy seam finishes

   - Turn and stitch. Stitch 1/4"
     from raw edge. Turn edge of
     seam allowance under on that
     stitching line and edge stitch.

   - Bind edges with double-fold 1/4"
     bias binding or "Finishing Touch"
     pre-folded lace. Slip over seam
     edge and topstitch in place. Use
     a contrasting color if you can't
     get a perfect match.

   - Hong Kong seam finish.
     Sew a 1 1/2" wide bias strip
     of lining fabric to edge of
     seam, right sides together, 1/4"
     from edge. Trim to 1/8". Turn
     lining to wrong side and top-
     stitch in well of seam from top
     side to catch in place. Trim.

2. How to cut a lining without a lining pattern.

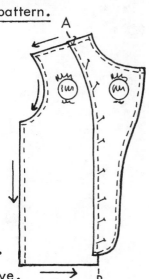

   - Front - Place facing pattern
     piece on top of front pattern
     piece. Cut from A to B. Pin
     mark facing stitching line.
     Remove pattern. Add 5/8"
     seam allowance - cut from
     B to A!
   - Back - Use back pattern piece.
     Allow a pleat as on page 39.
     Eliminate back facing from top
     of lining using same method as
     above for eliminating front facing.

   - Sleeve - Cut same as garment sleeve.

# Super Touches For a Custom Look!

## MACHINE BUTTONHOLES

They are great in children's coats and jackets where bound buttonholes may not be worth the time spent. Cord them so they won't stretch out.

Follow machine manual for buttonholes, but stitch them over cording or a heavy-weight thread. Leave a loop at the end. When buttonhole is completed pull on cording ends until loop disappears. With a hand sewing needle, bring loose cord ends to wrong side. Tie and clip.

## KEYHOLE BUTTONHOLES

If you have a keyhole attachment on your machine, use it for a sporty blazer look as designers are doing now. OR, find a tailor - they charge $1 to $2 per hand keyhole button-hole. A beautiful touch and worth every penny!

## BOUND BUTTONHOLES

Bound buttonholes are beautiful and durable and not hard to make once you develop a "system." We had to laugh when our artist Pricilla described a bound buttonhole - "It's just 3 lines". Well, its not quite as easy as an artist's concept but here are two favorite methods.

### Mark Carefully!

Using tracing paper or a lead pencil and a ruler, mark the center and ends of buttonhole on the interfacing side. Machine baste on these lines through interfacing and fashion fabric to transfer markings to right side. Use a contrasting color thread for easy-to-see markings.

NOTE: All horizontal buttonholes begin 1/8" toward edge from center front.

# BOUND BUTTONHOLE - SUSAN'S FAVORITE METHOD

NOTE: Always make a sample first to test the fashion fabric performance and buttonhole size (slip button through to make sure it fits!)

1. Mark fabric as shown on page 107.

2. Cut a strip of fabric the length of the buttonhole plus 1", and about 1 1/2" wide. Strip may be straight grain or bias.

NOTE: A faster way - Cut one long strip for all buttonholes. Snip apart as needed.

3. Corded buttonholes look best in everything but the very heaviest coatings, because they don't stretch or sink into the hole. To cord, fold strip in half, wrong sides together. Place small string or cording (preshrunk) in the fold.
Assemble invisible zipper foot so the needle hits just next to the cord. Tuck corded edge into zipper foot tunnel, machine stitch- should produce a 1/8" corded piping.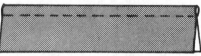

4. To aid stitching and reduce bulk, trim one raw edge to the exact width of the stitched cord.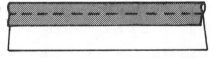

5. Center strip over vertical basting lines on the garment right side, with short raw edge against horizontal basting line. Stitch, on top of original stitching, using a short stitch, between the vertical markings. Back- stitch at each end.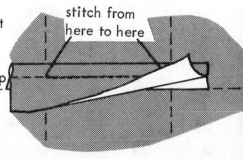

stitch from here to here

6. Place raw edge of second strip against the first strip raw edge. The two un-trimmed edges now for a "tent". Remember the tent! Stitch on top of original stitching between vertical markings.

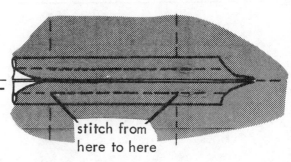

stitch from here to here

7. From wrong side, clip an X through all layers except buttonhole strips.

8. Turn strips to inside – tug lightly on strips to straighten lips and corners. Fold back fashion fabric exposing ends.

9. Stitch triangle ends as shown.

10. Finish facing as shown on page 113.

# BOUND BUTTONHOLE - PATI'S FAVORITE METHOD

1. Pin bias strips of matching lining (such as Poly-SiBonne or cotton organdy – even white organdy will hide after pressing) 1" longer than buttonhole and 1 1/2" wide on right side of garment centered over placement lines. (Do not use all-polyester or permanent press fabrics for bias strips. They resist pressing.)

2. Machine baste through center of lining. (Easiest when done from wrong side – just follow basting lines.)

3. Using small stitches, stitch a rectangle the length of the buttonhole and 1/4" wide (1/8" on either side of the center line). Use the edge of metal presser foot as a stitching guide. Start and stop stitching at "X" to avoid weak corners. Check each rectangle – they must be on grain, the same size, and have square corners. Remove basting.

center front

lining patch

4. From wrong side trim interfacing out of rectangle to eliminate bulk.

5. Clip rectangle to corners.

NOTE: Clip from center to corner to form larger wedges at each end.

6. Turn lining to wrong side to form "window". Press.

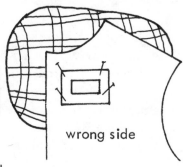

NOTE: An easy way to press... anchor lining by pinning to ham.

wrong side

7. Prepare lips by basting through the center of two pieces of fashion fabric, right sides together. Lips should be on straight of grain unless fashion fabric is plaid – then use bias.

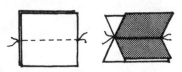

8. Center lips under window and baste in place. A speedy method for centering lips is to steam baste them in place with fusible web. Cut a piece of fusible web with a rectangle cut out of the center the size of buttonhole "window".

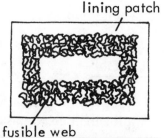

lining patch

fusible web

NOTE: To cut a window in the web, fold the rectangle in half and clip out a piece half the length of the buttonhole and 1/4" wide.

Place the web on the wrong side of buttonhole over the lining patch. "Steam baste" web in place by lightly steaming web until it becomes tacky and adheres to lining patch. (Do not touch iron to web !)

9. From right side, center lips under "window" and fuse using a press cloth. Lips will now stay in place without slipping while stitching.

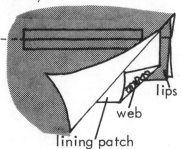

lips

web

lining patch

111

10. <u>Fold back fashion fabric</u> exposing sides. Using a zipper foot, stitch lining to lips. Do both long sides, then triangular ends. Stitch across triangle several times to anchor.

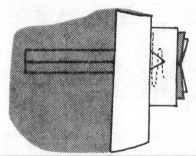

<u>NOTE</u>: For SPEED, do the same end of all the buttonholes at one time continuously.

11. <u>Trim and grade</u> back side of buttonhole. Hand catch stitch to interfacing. This is especially important for bulky fabrics.

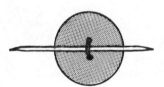

## BUTTONS

Sewing on buttons with a shank is especially important in tailoring due to the bulk of the fabric.

- Sew button on over a toothpick.

- Remove toothpick and wrap thread 5-10 times around shank. Knot.

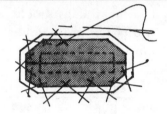

- Use a clear plastic backing button for added strength.

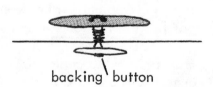

backing button

# EASY FINISH IN A FACING FOR A BOUND BUTTONHOLE

1. Pin facing in place smoothly over the back of buttonholes.

2. Put bias strips of lining on right side of facing over button-hole area. (Do this by "feel" from right side of garment and use 2" X 3" pieces of lining to make sure they cover button-hole area.)

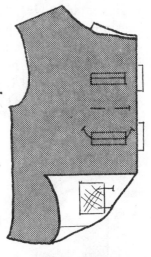

3. Stick pins straight down through ends of buttonholes.

4. Draw a pencil line on lining patch from pin to pin. This marks the center of the button-hole.

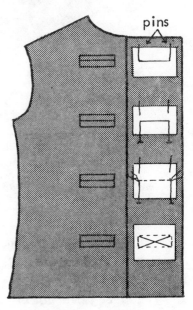

pins

5. Place two additional pins across ends of buttonholes and take first pins out.

6. Machine baste over center line from pin to pin.

7. Stitch a rectangle and clip to corners.

8. Turn lining patch to wrong side and press.

9. Steam baste a rectangle of fusible web to lining patch.

10. Fuse "window" in facing to back of buttonhole.

113

## SUPER-DUPER DOUBLE WELT POCKET

1. This is a double welt (usually at a slant when on a jacket). Notice welt ends are straight grain. Slip a lined pocket flap into a welt and it becomes a double welt pocket! Pocket flap ends are also straight grain.

2. If you could see through the jacket you would see the pocket lining at the same angle as your hand going in.

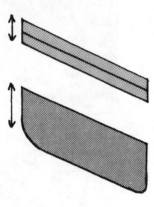

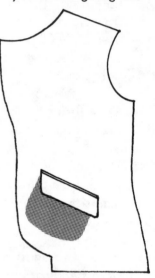

## DOUBLE WELT POCKET INSTRUCTIONS (for standard 6" pocket)

1. Welt – cut a rectangle of fashion fabric 3" wide and 8" long.

2. Lining – cut a piece of lining for pocket 8" wide and 15-18" long. Sew right side of lining to wrong side of welt piece, matching top raw edges. Stitch. Zig-zag over lower raw edge as shown.

3. Pellon stabilizer – cut a piece of Featherweight Pellon (not fusible) the same size as the welt.

4. Pencil 2 parallel lines the length of the Pellon, centered, 1/2" apart.

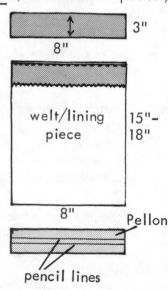

3"
8"

welt/lining piece | 15"-18"

8"

Pellon

pencil lines

5. On wrong side of jacket, mark pocket placement lines. End lines should be on straight of grain.

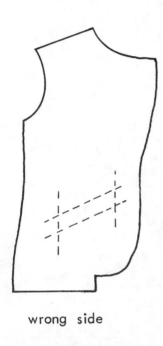

wrong side

6. On wrong side of jacket, place Pellon piece. Draw end lines on Pellon at placement markings on jacket, forming a "box". Stitch with small stitches around box. Start and stop stitching in center of pocket, not at a corner.

Pellon

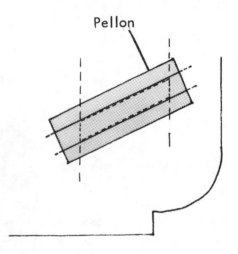

7. On right side of jacket, center welt/lining piece over straight lines. Pin in place.

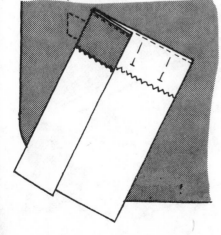

8. From wrong side, stitch on top of stitching lines on long sides of box only, stop at ends. Carefully back-stitch on top of last stitch.

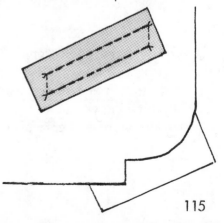

115

9. From wrong side, make 2 rows of basting stitches 1/4" above and below the box through all layers.

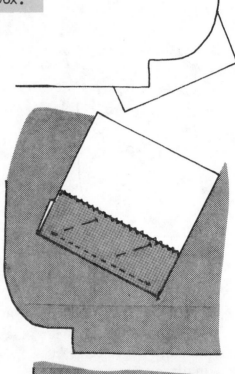

NOTE: Basting lines are always half the width of stitched box.

10. From right side, fold pocket up firmly against basting line and press. From wrong side, stitch again on lower long side of Pellon box - just follow previous stitch line and end exactly at end of box. Backstitch carefully. This will create the "welt."

11. On right side, fold upper part of welt down, press and pin. From wrong side, stitch on upper line of box. Backstitch at end carefully.

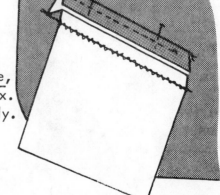

12. From right side of jacket,
    slash entire length of welts.
    DO NOT cut through to
    jacket yet. Remove basting
    threads.

13. From wrong side of jacket, cut
    through center of box to 3/4"
    from end. Cut to corner to
    middle of last stitch. Put your
    finger underneath as a guide to
    make sure you don't cut the welts.

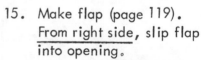

14. Pull everything through
    to wrong sides. Press.

15. Make flap (page 119).
    From right side, slip flap
    into opening.

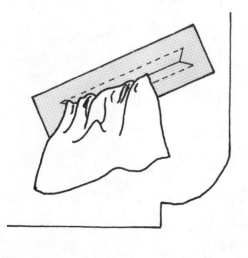

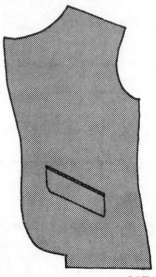

16. On wrong side, pin pocket flap to welt only.

17. On wrong side, stitch flap to top welt.

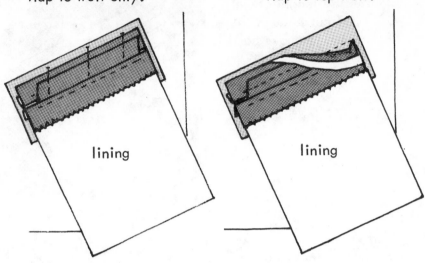

lining

lining

18. On wrong side, bring lining up and stitch across top welt on previous stitching line.

19. Secure triangles at ends of welt. Stitch sides and bottom of pocket as shown.

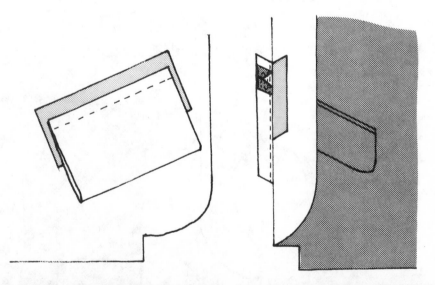

NOTE: Stitch pockets with a round bottom to prevent lint from collecting! Pockets may be shortened by stitching across bottom.

## POCKET FLAP

1. Cut flap.

2. Fuse lightweight fusible interfacing to wrong side of flap.

3. Cut lining – trim 1/8" off outer edges so lining won't show on finished flap.

4. Pin pocket and lining right sides together. Make sure edges match. Using 20 stitches per inch (so you can trim close) stitch lining to pocket.

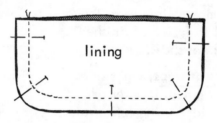

5. Pink seam allowance to 1/8" (or trim to 1/4", notch corners).

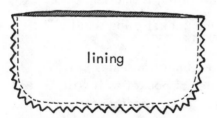

6. Turn and press.

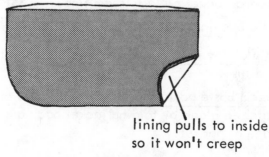

lining pulls to inside
so it won't creep

# TAILORED PATCH POCKET

1. Snip-mark cut-on facing fold line.

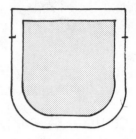

2. Trim 1/2" off seam allowances of interfacing. Fuse to wrong side of pocket.

3. Fold facing to wrong side at snips. Press.

4. Sew lining to pocket facing, right sides together. Machine baste for 2" at center. (Later, clip the basting to create an opening through which to turn the pocket.)

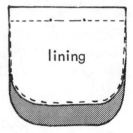

5. Trim 1/8" off outer edges of lining. This makes lining smaller so it will pull to inside of finished pocket and not show.

6. Fold pocket at snips, right sides together. Match all outer edges and pin in place using lots of pins. There will be a "bubble" in the pocket since lining is smaller.

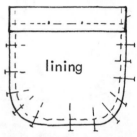

7. Stitch around pocket using small stitches.

8. Press lining seam allowances toward center of pocket so it will turn better. Trim, grade, notch, slash corners as necessary, or pink around pocket close to seam line.

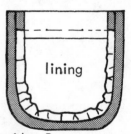

9. Clip opening and turn pocket to right side. Press.

10. Slip a piece of fusible web into the opening on wrong side and fuse.

11. Steam baste pocket to jacket with strips of fusible web. Slip stitch in place by folding jacket back and catching under edge of pocket.

# Special Tips for Tailoring

## SHAPING TRICKS

1. Underline with a hair canvas!  Susan owns a velveteen designer blazer that is underlined with a hair canvas.  She has worn it frequently for five years and it still looks new and never wrinkles.  Do not include hair canvas in the seams.  Either hand catch stitch edges to the fashion fabric seam line or zig-zag the canvas to a light weight underlining fabric.  Use a medium weight underlining for sleeves.

2. Underline with a fusible knit underlining like our friend Marta did in a beautiful wool gabardine overcoat for her husband.  It added body, wrinkle resistance and warmth - and a super look!

## PLAIDS

1. Cutting - For speedy and accurate plaid cutting, forget about pin matching the top and bottom layers when cutting double.  Instead, lay out pattern pieces on double layer of fabric, cut only the top layer.  Remove pattern and scrap fabric.  Slide cut piece until it matches the bottom plaid layer.  Cut!

   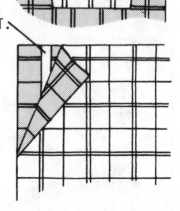

   T.B.T.

2. Sewing - Place Talon Basting Tape (T.B.T.) next to stitching line on right side of fabric.  Peel away protective paper.  Stick second layer of fabric on top, matching plaids.  Stitch next to T.B.T. - never through it.  Remove T.B.T. and press seam open.

# TOPSTITCHING

1. How to stitch straight - use the width of the presser foot as a guide. Also, try "Tapestitch" by Belding Lily. It is a premarked tape that is perforated in 1/8" to 3/4" widths. Choose the desired width, stick to fabric, stitch next to tape.

2. Thread - try silk buttonhole twist on natural fiber fabrics or the new long staple polyester topstitching thread on synthetic fabrics. Be sure to use a size 16 or 18 needle. To solve skipped stitches, try the no-fail Singer Yellow Band needle.

3. Decorative topstitching - try more than one row of stitching. We saw a beautiful designer jacket with three rows of silk twist topstitching. Try using a lighter shade for a dressier effect, a darker shade for a sportier effect, or a contrasting color for a very sporty look.

# MEN'S TAILORING

Pati has made lots of men's blazers and suits. She has tailored them like women's jackets except for the following:
- the back is softer, rarely underlined
- the buttonholes are made on the left jacket front
- keyhole buttonholes are used
- the Jacket-Package for menswear is great quick shaping in the chest and shoulder area. It includes a chest piece, a shoulder pad, and a sleeve head. These special menswear shaping accessories help us to achieve a professional tailor-made appearance with ease. Available in many fabric stores and departments or by mail from: Mid-Century Textile Corp., 202 W. 40th St., New York, N.Y., 10018, at $5.50.

If you decide to use traditional men's tailoring techniques, read one of the many good books on the subject. The techniques taught by Bev Smith are impeccable, she has spent years training with tailors and teaching men's tailoring. We have to thank her for teaching us the great double welt pocket! Her book may be ordered by writing for Men's Tailoring for the Home Sewer 1057 Landova Drive, Escondido, Calif. 92027. The cost is $5.95.

The best hint we can give you is to tell him the first jacket will turn out lousy - but to be patient. Then if it turns out great it's only a plus! It takes practice sewing for a body... yours or anyone elses!

## SHOULDER SHAPES

A shoulder shape smooths out the shoulder blade area and fills hollows in the upper chest. It is made of one layer of hair canvas and 2 to 4 layers of medium weight regular Pellon – buy 1/2 yard of each. It can be made into a shoulder pad by sandwiching layers of polyester fleece in between the layers of Pellon. You may add as many layers of Pellon or fleece as needed to even out the shoulder line – great for people with sloping shoulders. The shoulder shape is put into the jacket just before it is lined.

1. Use your jacket pattern – overlap shoulder seam lines of front and back pattern pieces and draw a one-piece shoulder shape from edge of armhole to neck seam, 7" long in back, 6" to 7" long in front. Cut a shape out of hair canvas as shown. Snip shoulder seam of canvas and mark front and back with pencil on canvas.

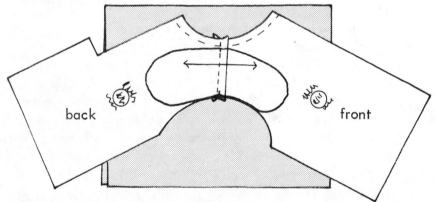

2. Cut triangles of Pellon as shown, snipping shoulder seam. Cut each triangle 1/4" smaller than the first on all but armhole edge and place canvas as shown.

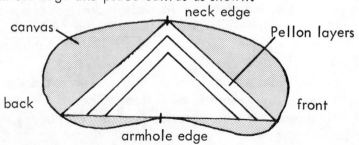

3. Stitch through shoulder seams on each unit.

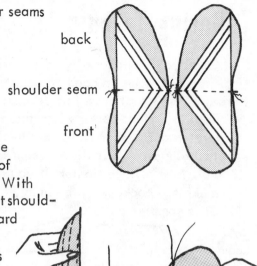

back

shoulder seam

front

4. Nifty Trick! Put curve into the shoulder shape while stitching layers of Pellon to the canvas. With Pellon on top, begin at shoulder seam and stitch toward end. Roll unit while stitching. This creates permanent slippage and forces the shoulder shape to curve. Stitch several rows 1" apart on both front and back sections.

5. Turn the jacket inside out and baste shoulder shape to jacket shoulder seam line.

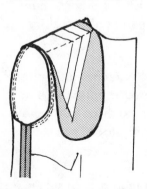

6. Turn jacket to the right sides, smooth shoulder shape in place and anchor with pins. How it looks right now is how it will look when you are finished. Leave pins in and baste shoulder shape from inside first to armhole seam allowance and then tailor baste to the interfacing.

125

# Tailoring Techniques. . .Other Uses

Once you've accomplished tailoring techniques, you'll find that they come in handy no matter what you are sewing. Here are a few that have lots of uses:

Taping – Slant pockets like those in trouser pants can stretch out of shape. To stay the edge , use two tailoring techniques. "Fell stitch" seam tape in place as shown. Pull tape a little tighter if you have a curvy figure to make the pocket hug the body. Topstitch edge when pocket is completed.

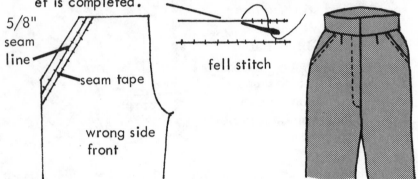

5/8"
seam
line

seam tape

fell stitch

wrong side
front

Taping may also be used on a "V" neck dress or vest to prevent "gaposis" of the neckline.

Lining – A lining can be a nice finish for any garment. The "jump hem" techniques is great in pant and skirt lining hems as well.

Bound Buttonholes – You may use this technique on any garment where you want a more durable buttonhole or where you can't match thread for a machine buttonhole. If you want an interesting effect in a plaid, make the lips on the bias.

Padded Sleeve Cap – We use this technique to set in sleeves in "hard-to-ease" Ultrasuede.

Interfaced Hems – You may interface the hem of a dress to make it hang better.

# OTHER BOOKS FROM PALMER/PLETSCH

Sewing Skinner® Ultrasuede® Fabric by Pati Palmer and Susan Pletsch.   80 pages of instructions to give you the "confidence to cut" into this luxurious fabric.  Revised edition copyright©1976.  $3.50

Pants for Any Body, by Pati Palmer and Susan Pletsch.  80 pages of easy-to-read instructions for fitting and sewing pants.  Revised edition copyright©1976.  $3.50

Mother Pletsch's Painless Sewing with Pretty Pati's Perfect Pattern Primer by Pati Palmer and Susan Pletsch.  136 pages of humor and hassle-free sewing tips.  Clear how-to-directions to make sewing fun, fast, and easy!  Copyright©1976.  $4.50

Sew a Beautiful Wedding by Gail Brown and Karen Dillon.  128 pages of the most current bridal how-to's.  Includes selecting a flattering pattern; how to sew with lace, velvet, satin, & sheers; simple-to-make headpieces and veils; bridal checklist.  Copyright©1980.  $4.95

SEW BIG!..a fashion guide for the fuller figure. In 128 pages SEW BIG! offers solutions to large size problems.  Photos, patterns, wardrobe accessory information.  Alteration instructions.  Copyright©1980.  $4.95

Books may be ordered through Palmer/Pletsch Assoc., PO Box 8422, Portland, OR. 97207. Please add 75¢ postage and handling. Slightly higher in Canada.  Canadian orders please pay in U.S. currency.

NOTES: